A SCIENTIFIC APPROACH
TO
DISTANCE RUNNING

by David L. Costill, PhD

Copyright   ©1979 by Track & Field News
All Rights reserved.

First Printing, January 1979
Second Printing, November 1979
Third Printing, September 1981

Production Staff: David Gleason, Grace Light, Debbie Sims.

Jacket Design: Ann Harris, Penny DeMoss.

Library of Congress Catalog Card Number: 78-68880
Standard Book Number: 0-911520-88-0

Printed in the United States of America

PHOTO CREDITS

p. 8 . . . . Don Chadez
p. 98 . . . . Gale Constable/Duomo
p. 111 . . . . John Hunt

TABLE OF CONTENTS

CHAPTER 1
PROFILE OF THE DISTANCE RUNNER

CHAPTER 2
PHYSIOLOGICAL RESPONSE DURING DISTANCE RUNNING

CHAPTER 3
ADAPTATIONS TO ENDURANCE TRAINING

CHAPTER 4
TRAINING AND PREPARATION FOR COMPETITION

PREFACE

Despite the rapid accumulation of scientific information during recent years, much of this new knowledge often remains too technical for practical application. The sciences of sport are no exception in this. There are many difficulties in bridging the gap between scientific observation and its assimilation into sports performance. One reason for this is that the scientist and the practitioner are often separated by a gulf in their perspectives. On the one hand, the scientist views his or her research as an end in itself and attempts to describe the results in terms understandable to other scientists. The coach and athlete, on the other hand, frequently lack a basic scientific knowledge of their sport and are ill-equipped to interpret the research that comes their way and translate it into improved performance.

It is hoped the following pages will provide a digest of the technical aspects of research that form the scientific basis for the concepts, both old and new, that affect the sport of distance running. Such an undertaking is certain to fall short of its mark, but if at best it offers some empirical basis for a runner to make decisions, it will have served its purpose.

There are many persons to whom I am indebted for their stimulating influence on my research, writing, and interest in distance running. Walley Guenther, Frank Nixon, and Bob Sawyers I thank for first showing me the exciting world of running by trying so hard and losing so often. Carl Maresh and Bill Fink were invaluable reviewers of the manuscript and can be blamed for all errors in the text. To Jo Hains and Judy Sparling I extend my admiration for their abilities to produce a perfect copy of this manuscript despite their many typing errors.

This book is dedicated to my family—Judy, Jill, and Holly—who have kindly tolerated my self-indulgence in research and running, two enjoyable ways to pass the days.

INTRODUCTION

One day in early 1976, soon after I had started doing preliminary research for *The Complete Book of Running,* I paid a call on David L. Costill at his laboratory on the campus of Ball State University in Muncie, Indiana. I didn't know Costill at the time, but I did know of his work, and I also knew that he had a reputation for being perhaps the foremost U.S. researcher into the physiological effects of distance running.

As soon as I set foot in his laboratory I understood why. Here was a complex array of equipment—a treadmill, a heat chamber and instruments so complex I could scarcely pronounce their names—all of them intended to search out the secrets of what happens to the human body when it runs. Here too, was a staff of physiological sleuths that had been carefully assembled to bring the most advanced knowledge to the inquiry.

Costill and I talked for a while as I took notes. I had already stood up to leave when he reached into a drawer, pulled out a manuscript, and said, "Here's something that might interest you; take it along." I have had enough manuscripts thrust unbidden into my hands over the years to have had the keen edge of anticipation blunted somewhat. I put Costill's manuscript into my briefcase and temporarily forgot about it.

A few days later on a train, I started reading it. It was a revelation. Here, in one place, were virtually all the scientific facts the average runner needs to know about the sport, most of them laboriously dug out by Costill and his staff in experiments on such champion runners as Frank Shorter, Don Kardong, and the late Steve Prefontaine. It was, I realized, beyond doubt the most important work of its kind. It has been of immeasurable importance to me, and I am glad that, at last, it will have the large readership it deserves.

I can, in fact, think of only one problem its publication creates: The runner who has studied it is sure to have an unfair advantage over his competitors who haven't.

—James F. Fixx

A Scientific Approach to Distance Running

TABLE OF FIGURES

PROFILE OF THE DISTANCE RUNNER

The popularity of distance running is quite recent. Scientists, however, have long been intrigued by the trained distance runner's unique ability to tolerate long endurance activity. In an effort to elucidate the qualities essential for superior performance in distance running, the physiologist has utilized the trained endurance runner as a key subject in his research. In the laboratory the distance runner serves as a unique model for studying the ultimate performance capacity and stress tolerance in man.

In this discussion, attempts are made to summarize the past and current research describing the anatomical, physiological, and psychological characteristics of successful distance runners. Although the investigations reported here are efforts to describe the unique qualities which typify top flight runners, it is logical to extrapolate some of these findings to all runners. Efforts are also made to illustrate how these research findings can be put to some useful application. Further, it is important to mention that the materials presented in this chapter represent aspects which are controlled by hereditary factors as well as the effects of acute and chronic endurance training.

PHYSICAL DIMENSIONS

After a recent lecture a man asked me, "How can I be a distance runner without looking like one?" This query was probably the result of the observation that many distance runners tend to be small and thin in physical dimension. As early as 1899 these qualities were recognized as necessary for successful marathon performance (Philadelphia Medical Journal, Vol. 3, page 12-33, 1933). Since that time detailed studies have reported more specifically the height, weight and body composition values of both male and female distance runners (11, 12, 20, 21, 46). Whereas early investigations suggested that "as the distance increases the runner becomes smaller," more recent studies fail to support this argument. For example, the average height for all the Boston Marathon champions from 1897 to 1965 was 170.4 centimeters (5-7¼—range: 154.9-188.9-centimeters) and winners from 1968 to 1975 have averaged 183.5 centimeters (6-¼—range: 179-188 centimeters) (33, 43); over the same period of time (1897-1975) the national average for height increased to about the same degree. Derek Clayton, who posted a marathon time of 2 hours 8 minutes 33 seconds, illustrates the current trend of taller men excelling in endurance running. His height is 188 centimeters (6-2), (13).

In a recent study of international and national caliber distance runners it is observed that the average height was 179 centimeters (5-10½), with an average body weight of roughly 65 kilograms (143 lbs). Although the physical stature of these runners is not significantly different from that of the average age- matched male, the body weight of these runners was substantially lower (minus 9.5 kilograms). It appears, therefore, that success in distance running is unaffected by body height, but that the mass carried by the individual may be crucial to performance. This is a logical interpretation since excessive body weight adds to the energy required to run and subsequently diminishes the athlete's potential for endurance.

Regardless of variations in structure, the successful distance runner is characterized by a low body fat content (11). Skinfold estimates of body fat of the distance runners at the 1968 U.S. Olympic marathon trials averaged 7.5% of total body weight. This is roughly 9% less than normally active men of a similar age (12). Recent underwater weight measurements for body fat of Frank Shorter, 1972 Olympic marathon champion and 1976

Olympic silver medalist, revealed a body fat content of only 1.6% (unpublished).

Since excessive body fat and bone structures serve as dead weight, it is easy to understand the advantage attributed the endurance runner with small bones and minimal body fat. One might ask the question, "What is the ideal body fat content for optimal distance running performance?" Current research findings do not present a clear answer for this question. However, data obtained from champion performers permit us to speculate that the highly trained runner may achieve greater success if his body fat is less than 5% of body weight. This may be true for the male runner, but it is difficult to interpret the literature in terms of the optimum body fat content for the female runner. There is some evidence to suggest that even highly trained female runners do not lower their body fat content below 7 or 8%. There are of course some exceptions to this point but, in general, we have observed that nationally-ranked female distance runners have a body fat content of roughly 8-10% of body weight.

No evidence is available to indicate that an excessively low body fat content can be injurious to one's health. Since we have observed a number of runners with less than 2.5% body fat (males), one would doubt that this poses a threat to either performance or health. In the female runner however, there is some suggestion that when the body fat content is reduced to less than 8 or 9% there is some interruption in the menstrual cycle. The mechanism underlying this problem has not been clearly defined. The condition of dysmenorrhea may reflect the high level of stress imposed on the female runner's physiology and may only be casually associated with the diminished body fat content.

If body fat measurements are to be performed on runners, they should be utilized only for longitudinal comparisons. The concept of making direct comparisons between athletes is unjustified. In most cases the error of measurement is too large to substantiate a reduction of body fat below 7 or 8%. However, it does seem prudent that regular monthly measurements be made of all runners' height, weight and body fat content. Such measurements are particularly important when one considers the growth and development patterns of young runners who are confronted with the stress of endurance training.

At present only limited information is available which describes other anatomical characteristics of male distance runners. In 1933, Boardman (4) reported that endurance runners have proportionally longer legs and shorter trunks per total height than the normal male. At the same time he observed that they have low and below average thigh and lower leg girth, narrow hips and shoulders and a shallow chest. It should be noted, however, that in 1933 the population of runners examined by Boardman was relatively small. A current examination of successful runners illustrates that they have many unique anatomical characteristics, but none distinguish them as exceptional or appear to provide a major performance advantage. One obvious characteristic of the distance runner is the deficiency in arm girth compared with chest size and leg development. This is supported by earlier studies and raises the question of a need for strength training programs for upper body development in the distance runner.

Although we have no empirical evidence for or against such a program, one can only examine the biological scheme of adaptations to endurance training to obtain an answer. In all systems placed under extreme stress there are major adaptations which compensate to insure an adequate capacity to tolerate subsequent stress. Thus, if upper body strength development were essential to success in endurance running then one would expect a natural adaptation to this system. In light of the small involvement of the upper body during distance running, it would seem that a strength training program is not essential for success in distance running. In fact, excessive upper body development might add to the runner's weight in a manner that would not positively contribute to the force needed in running. Thus, the runner looks as he does because he has developed a profile that is efficient for endurance performance.

AGING

Despite the public concept that sport success is terminated shortly after one leaves college, the distance runner has demonstrated that performance can be improved well into the third decade of life. Some early evidence demonstrated that both male and female endurance performers obtain their greatest success between the ages of 25 to 35 years of age. Tabulation of the ages of all distance runners in the 1964 Olympic games reveal a trend for the older runners to be more successful in the longer events (33). For example, the average age for the competitors in the 5000 meters, 10,000 meters and the marathon races were 27.0, 27.7, and 28.3 years respectively. The average age of all the Boston Marathon champions from 1897 to 1965 was 27.1 years with a range from 18 to 42 years (43).

Despite the degenerative influence of aging, many runners continue to compete successfully in long races until late in life. A classic example was Clarence DeMar, "Mr. DeMar-athon," who won his seventh Boston Marathon at the age of 42 years, placed seventh at the age of 50, and finished 78th in a field of 153 runners at the age of 65 (22, 43). The current international emphasis on endurance running has produced a considerable number of men older than 40 who have completed the marathon in less than 2 hours and 36 minutes at speeds averaging better than 16.1 km/hr (6 min/mile).

There have been few opportunities to examine the effects of aging on performance in distance running. Performance data obtained from three runners over many years of competition reveal a rapid decline in performance after the age of 32 years (Figure 1-1). This relationship between age and performance follows a similar pattern when the best world and American marathon times are plotted against age (Figure 1-2).

One obvious explanation for the decline in running performance after age 30-32 years is the gradual decline in the capacity to consume oxygen during exhaustive exercise (aerobic capacity). Figure 3 illustrates the relationship between age and maximal oxygen intake (VO_2 max) for trained distance runners and normally active men. More recent observations of trained endurance runners over the age of 60 have revealed exceptionally high VO_2 values (45, 55). Pollock, *et al.* (45) have reported a value of 61.1 ml/kg x minute for a 60-year-old runner who had performed a 2 hour 51.7 minute marathon. The highest VO_2 max values reported for a man over age 70 was that of 41.3 ml/kg x minute for a 72-year-old distance runner (55). Considering the aging influence depicted in Figure 3, it is apparent that endurance training strongly counteracts the effects of aging on cardiorespiratory endurance as measured by VO_2 max.

There is little doubt that the distance runner is at his best between 27 and 32 years of age. In light of current data, it is difficult to explain why runners 18 to 23 years of age do not perform equally as well, since many possess the physiological

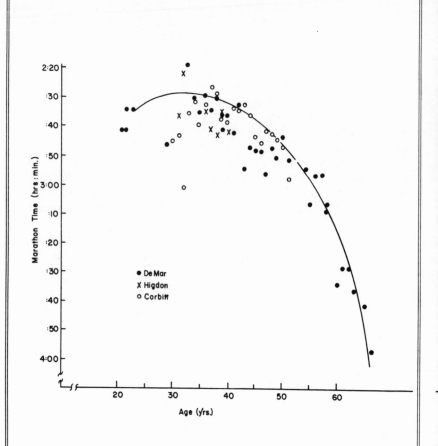

FIGURE 1-1.
EFFECTS OF AGING
ON MARATHON RUNNING PERFORMANCE.

Data obtained from plotting the careers of Clarence DeMar, Hal Higdon, and Ted Corbitt show a rapid decline in performance after age 32.

A Scientific Approach to Distance Running

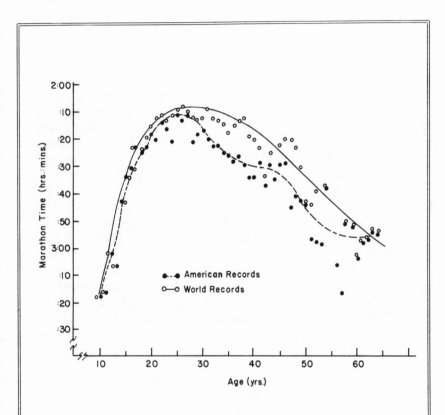

FIGURE 1-2.

RELATIONSHIP BETWEEN AGE AND THE BEST WORLD AND AMERICAN PERFORMANCES IN THE MARATHON.

When the best world and American marathon times are plotted against age, a similar pattern of decline is shown.

qualities generally associated with success in endurance performance. Perhaps future research will describe the subtle muscular adaptations that are achieved only with years of training.

SPEED AND STRENGTH

On most tests of strength and reaction time, distance runners tend to be below average (11, 53). A randomly selected group of male college students had a dominant hand grip strength of 53.2 kg (117.3 pounds), while 38 cross-country runners scored 48.1 kg (106.1 pounds). The same random male group averaged 53.1 cm (20.9 inches) on a vertical jump test, but the cross-country runners averaged only 47.2 cm (18.6 inches). One runner in this group could vertical jump only 34.3 cm (13.5 inches), but had sufficient speed to win the NCAA College Division 3-mile, 6-mile, and cross-country championships (11). Cureton (20) concedes that endurance runners are not usually strong (gross strength) but are normal when strength is determined in relation to their body weight.

The observation that distance runners lack explosive leg strength is an interesting one and warrants additional comment. In order to shed some light on this problem let me cite a case study. In 1968 we tested Lou Castagnola, a 2:17 marathoner. At that time he had a maximal oxygen uptake (VO_2 max) of 72.4 ml/kg x minute and a vertical jump of only 29.2 cm (11.5 inches). Following the 1968 U.S. Olympic marathon trial he terminated all training. Three years later we re-examined him and found his VO_2 max had declined to 47.6 ml/kg minute. His vertical jump, on the other hand, increased to 51.5 cm (20.3 inches), a 76% increase despite his detrained status. This suggests that endurance running impairs leg speed and explosive power. Although the mechanism for this response remains obscure, recent evidence concerning the recruitment of muscle fibers and the specificity of endurance training suggests that there may be a selective reduction in the number of motor units available for the distance runner to perform the vertical jump. It is possible that the fiber composition and neurological innervation of the endurance athlete's muscle precludes the type of quick response required for explosive jumping. Additional attention will be given to this area in the discussion on muscle fiber composition.

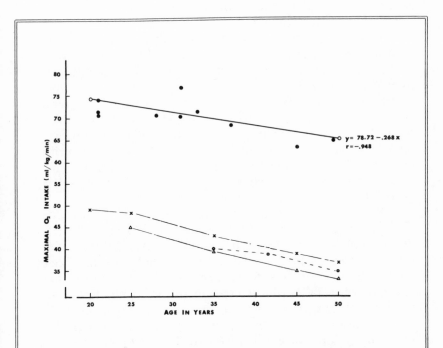

FIGURE 1-3.

**MAXIMAL OXYGEN UPTAKE AT VARIOUS AGES FOR
NORMALLY ACTIVE MEN (OPEN CIRCLES)
AND MARATHON RUNNERS (CLOSED CIRCLES).**

*Recent observations of runners over 60 show that endurance
training strongly counteracts the effects of aging on
cardiorespiratory endurance as measured by VO_2 max.*

CARDIAC CHARACTERISTICS

It is generally agreed that the cardiovascular system of the endurance trained athlete is one of the prime contributors to successful distance running.

In 1962, Smith *et al.* (51) studied the electrocardiograms of marathon runners competing in the British Commonwealth Games. They noted a high voltage of the QRS complex and somewhat enlarged T-waves. Similar findings were reported by Arstila and Koivikko (1) in 1966. Their electrocardiographic and vectorcardiographic studies of 46 endurance athletes showed that a large proportion had cardiac hypertrophy. Similar findings of ventricular hypertrophy have been verified by x-ray shadow estimates of heart size (20). Paavo Nurmi, seven times Olympic champion, was found to have a heart nearly three times normal size (4).

Resting electrocardiographic recordings have been utilized clinically to diagnose abnormalities in the electrical transmission of impulses across the heart muscle. Until recently these methods were seldom utilized to examine healthy, highly trained distance runners. Such examinations tend to place some doubt on the validity of using the electrocardiogram to diagnose cardiac impairments in distance runners. Measurements of the ST segment have been generally used to identify individuals with impairments in coronary blood flow. Gibbons *et al.* (27) recently examined 20 elite distance runners and noted that 25% of these athletes exhibited significant changes in the ST segment which would be suggestive of coronary heart disease. Although ST segment depressions immediately following exercise have been previously reported in distance runners, these observations are rare and generally occur in populations that include runners in their 40's and 50's. Evidence of coronary heart disease in this age group would seem probable. None of Gibbons subjects, who exhibited ST segment depression, had any known cardiovascular disease. Further, they experienced no symptoms suggestive of heart disease, nor any significant abnormalities on additional cardiovascular examination that would suggest an impairment in coronary blood flow. Although no invasive studies were attempted to resolve cardiac status of these runners, it is unlikely that the ST segment depression seen could be interpreted in the same manner as would be done for the general population. These and other apparently non-functional abnormalities in the electrocardiograph lead us to doubt that electrocardiographic interpretations in exercising endurance athletes can be interpreted with the same criteria as that utilized in a clinical environment.

An interesting difference between older and younger endurance athletes has been observed. The former exhibit more electrocardiographic signs of left ventricular hypertrophy than of right ventricular hypertrophy, while the latter show left ventricular hypertrophy less frequently than right ventricular hypertrophy. The predominance of right ventricular hypertrophy in young athletes may be evidence of comparatively more right-side work during the first years of training, after which the left ventricle gains comparatively greater weight and becomes dominant.

In addition to signs of hypertrophy, several investigators have observed intraventricular conduction defects among trained runners (26, 28, 52). While such findings might cause considerable alarm when observed in untrained middle-aged men, these abnormalities have little medical significance when occurring in young, otherwise symptom-free athletes.

Post-mortem examination of the distance runner's heart is seldom possible. However, findings in the case of Clarence DeMar, who competed in over 1000 long-distance races during his life, revealed a significantly enlarged heart. In 1958, DeMar was diagnosed as having peritoneal carcinomatosis, but he continued to train within two weeks of his death. His heart weighed 340 grams (normal male heart is 300 grams). The left ventricular wall was 18 mm thick (normal = 10-12 mm), and the right 8 mm (normal = 3-4 mm). The valves were normal, but the coronary arteries were estimated to be two or three times normal size. The very large coronary vessels alone, other things being equal, would insure an adequate oxygen supply to cardiac muscle when the demands were great. This probably reduced to a minimum the need for hypertrophy of the heart which was still observed. The evidence in DeMar's case, after 49 years of strenuous physical training, was one of notable compensatory changes.

Caution should be used in generalizing about cardiac hypertrophy in distance runners. A major criticism in reporting heart sizes among endurance athletes is that in no instance was heart size determined before the athlete engaged in training. This is important since the range of normal heart size varies even in individuals of the same height, weight, and age.

Bramwell and Ellis (7) have suggested that some persons are born with a heart distinctly larger than the average, which could give them a potential advantage in endurance activities.

BLOOD AND CIRCULATORY ASPECTS

Although many distance runners possess a markedly lower resting heart rate than age-matched untrained counterparts, the volume of blood ejected from the heart with each beat (stroke volume) has been reported to be nearly double the normal value (31). Since a large stroke volume is the product of ventricular enlargement there is more complete emptying with each ventricular contraction. Consequently, the endurance athlete's heart accomplishes its work at rest and during exercise with considerably greater efficiency than the average person's heart.

This distinct difference in ventricular size is illustrated in Figure 4. Here are shown the chest x-rays for two men of similar age, height, and weight. The lateral dimension of the marathon runner's heart (15.5 cm) is roughly 52% greater than the normally active-inactive man. Standing at rest the untrained man had a heart rate of 78 beats per minute, while the marathoner had a rate of only 32 beats per minute. If we assume that under these circumstances the men had similar cardiac outputs, then the marathon runner must have a stroke volume nearly 2.5 times greater than the untrained man.

Although it is true that there are a variety of factors (emotional, environmental, previous activity, etc.) that can influence the resting heart rate, distance runners have been known to possess exceptionally low basal (early morning) and resting heart rates. Under very controlled conditions, resting and basal heart rates have been found to correlate quite highly ($r = -0.61$ and -0.65, respectively) with cross-country running performance (11). However, one must remember that both basal and resting heart rates are significantly influenced by training, which seems to be the primary cause for bradycardia among athletes trained for endurance competition. Since the athlete can deliver the same cardiac output at a lower heart rate during exercise, this permits a greater period of diastole (heart rest). Thus the heart has more time to fill with returning blood (venous return) and for blood to flow through the coronary arteries.

Various circulatory measurements and physical fitness tests have been used to identify potential endurance running

20

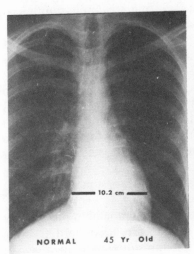 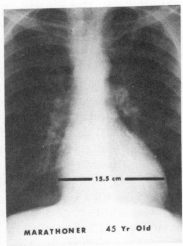

FIGURE 1-4.
CHEST X-RAY OF A MARATHONER AND A NORMALLY ACTIVE MAN. MEASURED LINES DENOTE HORIZONTAL WIDTH OF HEART SHADOW.

The lateral dimension of the marathon runner's heart is roughly 52% greater than the normally-active/inactive man. Assuming similar cardiac outputs, the marathon runner's stroke volume is nearly 2.5 times greater than that of the untrained man.

ability. For example, trained cross-country runners score significantly higher than other trained athletes on the Harvard Step Test and Bruce Physical Fitness Index (11, 44). Also, as one might anticipate, treadmill running time to exhaustion has been found to correlate quite highly with distance running success (20). Probably the best single circulatory parameter for prediction of distance running time is the percentage of maximal heart rate (% HR max) during treadmill running at 268m/min (10 mph). As can be seen in Figure 5, this measure correlates highly with the time for a 10-mile run.

Several studies have shown that indirect blood pressures recorded at rest are not significantly related to endurance capacity (11, 20). Since training has been found to lower an athlete's diastolic blood pressure, it is not surprising to find studies which report normal systolic pressures (120-122 mmHg) and low diastolic values (50-63 mmHg) among college cross-country runners (11). Brachial pulse waves, as measured by a heartometer, have no more value in predicting cross-country running time than can be assumed from the resting pulse rate (41).

Since most runners are aware that hemoglobin plays a key role in oxygen transportation, some worry that hard training may result in blood cell destruction and subsequent anemia. Let us consider some basic points relative to blood cell production in the training athlete. In terms of the ratio of red blood cells to whole blood (hematocrit), distance runners do not differ significantly from untrained men. That is not to say that untrained men have the same number of circulating red cells as the distance runner. To the contrary, endurance training elicits an increase in plasma volume. As a result, the trained runner possesses a greater number of red blood cells with a normal hematocrit. It should be pointed out that during repeated days of heavy training, plasma volume may increase 15-30% as a result of renal sodium conservation and water retention. This produces a dilution of the circulating red cells. It is not uncommon, therefore, to observe unusually low hematocrits (39%) and hemoglobin (14.0 g/100 ml) concentrations in trained distance runners. Since most runners still have an enlarged volume of red blood cells, it seems inaccurate to describe them as anemic, yet we do not know what influence these low hemoglobin concentrations might have on the oxygen carrying capacity of blood during exercise.

There are of course some exceptions and variations in the production and loss of red blood cells. Some investigators have

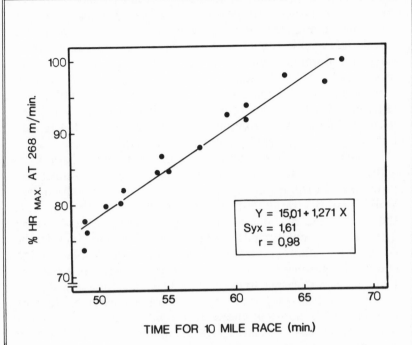

FIGURE 1-5.
RELATIONSHIP BETWEEN PERFORMANCES IN A 10-MILE
(16.1 KM) RACE AND THE PERCENTAGE OF THE
RUNNER'S MAXIMAL HEART RATE RECORDED
WHILE RUNNING AT 268 M/MIN.

Running on a treadmill at 10 mph correlates highly with one's time in a 10-mile run.

reported an increase rate of red cell destruction during heavy endurance exercise, but it is generally agreed that this is a rather unusual occurrence and provides an unlikely explanation for lowering hemoglobin and red cell concentrations in whole blood. The female runner who experiences excessive menstrual flow may develop a mild state of anemia. The body's normal mechanism of red cell production should, of course, compensate for this red cell loss. Nevertheless, hemoglobin and red cell volumes are lower in females than in males. This may mean a slightly lower oxygen carrying capacity for the female but this point has never been clearly elucidated.

There are those who contend that participation in endurance type activities provide some protection against the problems of cardiovascular disease and degeneration with aging. While there is little definitive evidence to support this concept, there are some risk factors to coronary disease which may be offset by continued regular endurance training. One such factor is the alternation in the blood fat (lipid) profile seen in the endurance performer. For the most part, endurance training tends to lower plasma triglyceride values and initiates a shift in the composition of lipoproteins toward a greater content of high density lipoprotein cholesterol. Since both of these factors have been closely correlated with the incidence of heart disease, this change in the plasma lipid profile is suggestive of a reduction in the risk of heart disease. Although physical training seems to have little effect on plasma cholesterol concentrations, distance runners are generally characterized by a low level of cholesterol. This may, however, be a result of their high metabolic turnover of ingested fuels or the fact that they seldom ingest foods high in cholesterol.

Since heavy endurance training tends to alter many of the constituents of plasma it is important that concentrations of most items be viewed cautiously. One example is the change in serum enzymes following prolonged exercise. Clinically, the enzyme lactic dehydrogenase (LDH) is used as an indicator of cardiac and soft tissue damage. At the same time, this enzyme is found in rather high concentrations in the blood following a long endurance run. These and other enzymes should be carefully examined and seldom interpreted in the same light as samples obtained under clinical conditions.

PULMONARY CHARACTERISTICS

A runner's vital capacity, the maximal volume of gas that can be expelled from the lungs by forced effort following a maximal inspiration, can be significantly enlarged with years of training (5). It is not surprising, therefore, to find that distance runners are significantly above average for this measure. One study observed vital capacities (BTPS) of approximately 5.71 liters for 17 cross-country runners (1). The mean vital capacity for average, untrained men of the same age is 4.8 liters (8). When computed on the basis of body size (height, weight, or body surface area), distance runners score even higher as a result of their small vertical and lateral dimensions.

Training for distance running develops tremendous respiratory muscle stamina and strength. Maximum breathing capacity (MBC) is the maximum volume of air that can be breathed per minute (9). While the normal male is said to have an MBC of from 125 to 170 liters per minute, a group of 10 college cross-country runners had a mean MBC of 207.5 liters per minute (6). One might theorize that well-trained distance runners have developed exceptional endurance in their respiratory musculature and/or reduced respiratory resistance which might enable them to carry on external respiration during heavy exercise without over-taxing their respiratory musculature. During exhaustive running, highly trained distance runners have been able to breathe over 120 liters per minute for more than twenty minutes (10). Among untrained men such a large minute volume is normally attained only during the final minutes of exercise, and can be maintained for only a very short period.

Recent measurements of pulmonary function among marathon runners have revealed a significantly higher carbon monoxide diffusing capacity than was predicted for these men (37). This capacity for gas to diffuse more rapidly between the alveoli and pulmonary blood is presumably facilitated by an increase in total body hemoglobin (35). This finding is compatible with the superior oxygen transport system developed by the trained distance runner.

AEROBIC CAPACITY

Since the early work of Hill and Lupton (32), exercise physiologists have associated the limits of human endurance with the ability to consume larger volumes of oxygen during exhaustive effort. This point is well documented in distance runners (2, 11, 18, 19, 40, 48, 50). While the normally active 20-year-old male has a maximal oxygen uptake (VO_2 max) of roughly 44-47 ml/kg x minute, trained distance runners commonly have values in excess of 70 ml/kg x minute. In a recent (1974) series of studies among top U.S. distance runners, Steve Prefontaine,, American record holder for the 5000 meters, recorded a VO_2 max of 84.4 ml/lg x minute.

Although this ability to consume, transport, and utilize large volumes of oxygen is a crucial factor for distance running success, it frequently fails to predict the winning performer when a group of homogenously talented runners compete (16). That is to say, top flight runners may have similar running performances but have markedly different VO_2 max values. This is demonstrated in the case of Frank Shorter and Steve Prefontaine. Both men have posted times of roughly 12:52 for 3 miles. Yet, the highest VO_2 max value recorded for Shorter is only 71.4 ml/kg x minute, 13 ml/kg x minute less than Prefontaine. It is, however, interesting to note that Shorter's VO_2 max value is quite similar to the value reported for Derek Clayton, one of history's best marathon performers (13). Despite Clayton's ability to run at an average speed of 328 m/min. (4:54 sec/mile) for 42 km, his VO_2 max was only 69.7 ml/kg x minute. These data make it apparent that a high VO_2 max in itself does not guarantee a fast performance in marathon competition.

In addition to the actual size of the aerobic capacity, other factors are instrumental in determining a winning performance. One such factor is the ability to utilize a large fraction of one's VO_2 (% VO_2 max) for prolonged periods. Although most distance runners employ about 75-80% of their aerobic capacity during the marathon, Clayton and Shorter have been estimated to use 86 to 90% of VO_2 max (10, 13,16). Work performed at this high percentage customarily results in a large accumulation of lactic acid: a response to insufficient oxygen delivery to the working muscles. In one series of experiments Clayton was required to perform a 30 minute treadmill run at 328m/minute (4:54 sec/mile), a pace which equalled his best marathon performance (13). Heart rate responses during the run were constant at 167 beats/min., compared to his maximal heart rate of 188 beats/min. Venous blood lactate values at 10 and 30 minutes of the run were 2.1 and 2.3 mmoles/liter, respectively,

A Scientific Approach to Distance Running

not much above his pre-exercise value of 1.3 mmoles/liter. This ability to exercise at a high % VO_2 max for prolonged periods without accumulating lactic acid remains unexplained. However, it has been speculated that these qualities are functions of muscular adaptations to endurance training (18). Additional attention will be given to these factors in a later discussion.

MUSCLE FIBER CHARACTERISTICS

A runner's ability to maintain a fast pace during competition depends to a large part on the muscles' ability to generate energy and tension. Individual differences observed in performance can in some ways be related to the characteristics of the runners' leg muscles. Recent advances in surgical techniques have made it possible to obtain samples of human skeletal muscle and to subsequently assess the compositions and endurance characteristics of muscle. Microscopic and biochemical analyses are used to identify various metabolic properties of the muscle sample, which are then assumed to be representative of the whole muscle. One of the most interesting characteristics yet identified with these techniques is the type of muscle fibers which make up the biopsy sample. The following discussion focuses on the fiber "types" and their relationship to endurance performance.

The microscopic photograph presented in Figure 6 demonstrates the two fiber types found in human skeletal muscle. The unstained fibers are associated with "fast" contractile properties of the muscle fiber and are thus termed fast twitch (FT). The darkly stained fibers are relatively slow in contractile rate and are referred to as slow twitch (ST). In general, ST fibers demonstrate a higher oxidative (aerobic) and lower glycolytic (anaerobic) potential than do FT fibers.

There is substantial evidence which demonstrates that successful endurance athletes have relatively more ST than FT fibers in their muscles (14, 15, 17, 30). World-class sprinters, on the other hand, have leg muscles that are composed predominantly of FT fibers (15, 30). As can be seen in Figure 7, male and female track athletes have varied % ST fibers in their gastrocnemius muscle. Recent studies of top flight U.S. distance runners revealed that some had greater than 90% of their gastrocnemius muscle composed of ST fibers (17). Although the % ST fibers effectively discriminates between good and elite distance runners, fiber composition alone is a poor predictor of endurance running success.

Previous studies have shown that training may increase the oxygen utilizing capacity of skeletal muscle, but there is little evidence to suggest that the percentage of slow twitch and fast twitch fibers changes with endurance training. One exception to this case is the fact that the sub type of fast twitch fibers (FT_a and FT_b) may show some modification. The FT_a fibers are generally described as being a bit more oxidative in their metabolic capacity than the ST_b fibers. In the untrained individual the percentage of FT_a and FT_b is about the same. With endurance training, however, the FT_b fibers begin to take on the characteristics of the FT_a fibers. This would suggest that these fibers are more heavily used in endurance training and do in fact gain greater oxidative ability. The scientific significance of this change in the type FT_a and FT_b fibers is not fully understood. It should be noted that a discussion of fast twitch and slow twitch merely describes the contractile characteristics of these muscle cells, and does not directly indicate their endurance qualities.

With endurance training it is well known that fast twitch fibers begin to take on the endurance characteristics of slow twitch fibers. Thus, under microscopic examinations, the well-trained distance runners' muscles will appear highly oxidative and will possess a large percentage of slow twitch fibers. Recent investigations have shown that the ratio of slow twitch to fast twitch fibers remains unchanged as a result of 4-6 months of training in young (11-13 years) and adult males (24, 29). This leads us to conclude that individual differences in the percentage of slow twitch fibers are a result of natural endowment and not a function of training adaptation.

The cross-sectional area of muscle fibers varies markedly among elite distance runners, although this may simply reflect the variations in fiber length and contractile status at the time of biopsy. However, on the average, ST fibers are generally larger (+22%) than FT fibers in elite distance runners' gastrocnemius (14). Saltin (49) has proposed that training for endurance or strength may result in selective enlargement (hypertrophy) of the ST and FT fibers, respectively.

These microscopic observations demonstrate that the musculature of elite distance runners is characterized by a high % ST fibers. This fractional composition of muscle appears fixed and unaffected by training, suggesting that it may be

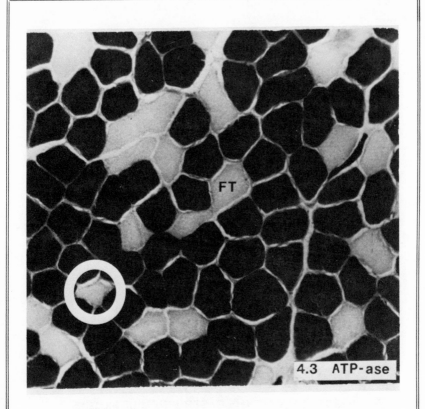

FIGURE 1-6
**MICROSCOPIC VIEW OF SKELETAL MUSCLE FROM THE
GASTROCNEMIUS OF A WORLD-CLASS DISTANCE
RUNNER (STEVE PREFONTAINE).**

*The untrained fibers are associated with "fast" contractile
properties of the muscle fiber and are termed* fast twitch *(FT).
The darker fibers are slower in contractile rate and are termed*
slow twitch *(ST). In general, ST fibers demonstrate higher aerobic
and lower anaerobic potential than do FT fibers.*

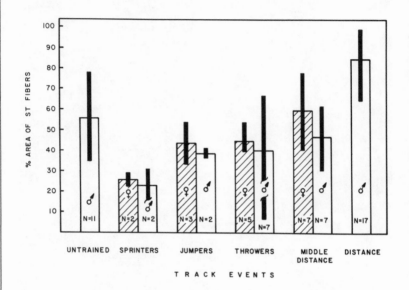

FIGURE 1-7.

**PERCENTAGE OF THE GASTROCNEMIUS MUSCLE
AREA COMPOSED OF SLOW TWITCH FIBERS IN
UNTRAINED MEN AND TRAINED TRACK ATHLETES.**

*Male and female track athletes have varied percentages of ST
fibers in their gastrocnemius muscle. Though the % ST fibers can
distinguish between good and elite distance runners for both
sexes, fiber composition alone is a poor predictor of distance
running success.*

possible to identify individuals with endurance potential early in life.

METABOLIC ASPECTS OF MUSCLE

Muscular adaptations to exercise are generally characterized by an enhanced capacity to produce energy (ATP) for muscular work (34). This is, in part, attributed to an increase in the number and size of "power-house" like units (mitochondria) responsible for oxidizing fuels. In order to speed the rate of energy production and to perform this task efficiently, mitochondria employ specialized proteins called enzymes. Since the mitochondrial enzymes require the availability of oxygen for their operation they are referred to as oxidative enzymes. On the other hand, the anaerobic (without oxygen) processes of metabolism are performed in the sarcoplasm (fluid portion of the cell) and require specific glycolytic enzymes. As their name implies, these enzymes are involved in the breakdown of glycogen but do not require the presence of oxygen. There appears to be some question as to the adaptability of these enzymes to training.

Comparative studies have shown a positive relationship between the ability of a muscle to perform prolonged exercise and the activity of its oxidative enzymes. This is compatible with the finding that the running musculature of elite distance runners has nearly 3.5 times more oxidative enzyme activity (succinic dehydragenase) than that of untrained men (15). Figure 8 suggests that at least part of the distance runners' enhanced capacity for oxygen consumption is determined by the oxidative potential of their running musculature. Since these runners possess more ST fibers, which generally show a high oxidative potential, one might be led to conclude that distance runners are endowed with a greater capacity for adaptation to endurance training. Current research findings do not support this concept, however, since little relationship has been found between % ST fibers and SDH activity (15). Certainly endurance training can enhance the oxidative capacity of the FT fibers, which probably explains the high oxidative enzyme activity that has been found in trained gastrocnemius muscle containing only 24% ST fibers (14).

One of the factors responsible for exhaustion during prolonged endurance exercise is the rapid depletion of glycogen from the exercising muscle. Physical training provides some adaptations which enable the muscle to conserve glycogen and substitute fat for energy during competition. The apparent advantage in performing prolonged endurance runs in training is to modify and enhance the muscles' capacity to burn fat and to reinforce the mechanisms responsible for the breakdown and release of fat from the fat cells. Both of these processes permit the muscle to oxidize fat at the greater rate and thereby spare the use of glycogen. Recent studies in our laboratory have demonstrated that the gastrocnemius muscle is 7 times more capable of burning fat after marathon training than would normally be expected in the untrained muscle. The degree to which the muscle adapts for fat oxidation depends for the most part on the volume of work imposed on the muscle. Thus, we now have evidence to substantiate why it is essential for the endurance runner to perform extremely long runs in training and to log 80-120 miles per week.

In terms of glycolytic enzyme activities, distance runners' muscles are similar to the untrained muscle of sedentary men. Although some investigators have reported that endurance training can produce an 85% increase in selected glycolytic enzyme activities, the stimulus for biosynthesis of these enzymes (e.g., PFK) may necessitate exercise of greater intensity than that commonly employed during training for distance running (24). Future research is needed to demonstrate the relationship between both glycolytic and oxidative enzyme activities and variations in distance running performance. Only then will we fully understand the physiological significance of these specialized muscle proteins.

PSYCHOLOGICAL PROFILE

A few studies have attempted to evaluate the intellectual or emotional characteristics of distance runners. In 1955 Husman (36) studied the aggressive nature of various groups of college athletes and non-athletes; boxers (N-9), wrestlers (N-8), cross-country runners (N-9), and a control group (N-17). The Rosenzweig Picture-Frustration Study, Murray's Thematic Apperception Test, and a 20-sentence completion test were used to measure aggression. It was concluded that the cross-country runners tended to be more outwardly aggressive (extrapunitively) than the boxers. The runners were also found to be extrapunitive and less impunitive than the control group members, showing aggression against persons and objects in the

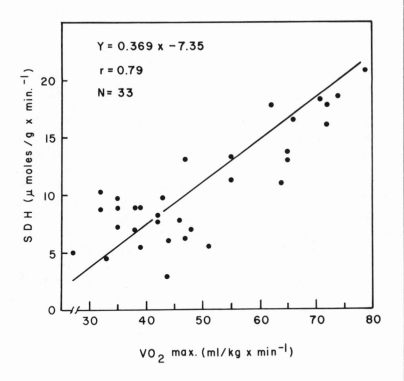

FIGURE 1-8.
**RELATIONSHIP BETWEEN MAXIMAL OXYGEN
UPTAKE AND THE OXIDATIVE ENZYME ACTIVITY
(SDH) OF THE GASTROCNEMIUS.**

*It appears that at least part of the distance runners' enhanced
capacity for oxygen consumption is determined by the oxidative
potential of the running muscles.*

environment more than the control group.

Studies conducted in 1970 on nine elite marathon runners revealed that they did not differ significantly from normal limits on tests of extraversion-introversion, neuroticism-stability or depression (42). However, they scored appreciably lower than the norm for anxiety. For the most part, these findings agree with the observations made by Lakie (39). He reported no personality differences among basketball, football, tennis, golf, wrestling, or track participants.

Recent studies by Morgan, *et al.* on 24 elite distance runners reveal that elite marathon runners are very similar from a psychological standpoint to middle-long distance runners as well as world-class athletes in other sports such as wrestling. It was also concluded that elite marathon runners are characterized by positive mental health from an effective standpoint. This positive act is regarded as a consequence of training and competition, since these world-class athletes resemble the general population on most psychological traits. The major distinguishing psychological characteristics of the elite marathoners were the ability to monitor their physiological systems and to have an "effort sense" in pacing themselves during competition.

SEX DIFFERENCES

Only in recent years have efforts been made to study the difference between male and female distance runners. Table 1 presents mean data for groups of world-class male and female distance runners. In contrast to their male counterparts, trained female distance runners have significantly more body fat (54). This may be misleading since several elite female runners have relatively the same body fat content (5 - 6%) as world-class male marathon runners. However, Wilmore *et al.* (54) have reported a mean body composition of 15.2% fat for eleven national and international caliber female runners (24-37 years of age). This is nearly three times as great as an elite group of age-matched male runners (avg. = 5.6% of body weight). In terms of either gross weight or fat free body weight, men are substantially heavier.

Although the VO_2 max values for female (59.1 ml/kg x min) runners are significantly greater than those for normally active age-matched women (39 ml/kg x min), they are markedly lower than those reported for their male runner counterparts (Table 1). This fact alone probably accounts for the differences observed in distance running performance between men and women. The highest VO_2 max values presently reported in the literature for male and female distance runners are 84.4 and 71.1 ml/kg x min. respectively. At least part of the difference in VO_2 max between the sexes can be attributed to variations in circulatory capacity for oxygen transport.

Table 1-1 Mean − SE characteristics of male (M)
and female (F) world class distance runners

Sex	No.	Age (yrs)	Ht (cm)	Wt (kg)	LBW (kg)	Fat (%)	VO_2 max (ml/kg x min)	HR max (bts/ min)
M 20		26	177.0	63.1	59.5	5.6	76.9	198
		(±0.6)	(±1.4)	(±1.1)	(±0.9)	(±0.6)	(±0.8)	(±1.6)
F 22		32	169.4	57.2	48.1	14.2	59.1	180
		(±1.4)	(±2.7)	(±2.0)	(±1.1)	(±2.4)	(±2.0)	(±2.7)

Raven *et al.* (47) have reported a maximal cardiac output (Q max) of 27.6 liters/min. for a 57 kg champion female distance runner. It is not uncommon for male runners and other endurance athletes to have Q max values in excess of 35 liters/min. (23,25). An interesting observation seen in Table 1 is the significant difference in maximal heart rates for the male and female distance runners. At present we cannot explain the functional significance for this difference.

In terms of muscle fiber composition, little difference has been found between male and female track athletes within various events. Although few muscle biopsies have been obtained from elite female distance runners, current evidence suggests that they too are endowed with a large proportion of slow twitch muscle fibers (14), but that their muscle fibers are a bit smaller in cross sectional area. Muscle samples obtained from the gastrocnemius of female middle distance runners reveal a larger percentage of ST fibers than a similar group of male runners (Figure 7). This difference is probably explained by the fact that in the past there have been few long distance races for women. As a result, the women demonstrating the greatest endurance were selected to participate in the 800 and 1500 meter races. On the other hand, men showing similar performance aptitude were channeled into the longer running events. Consequently, these data may simply reflect a choice of events based on proven success in endurance competition.

It has been observed that females frequently have difficulty in competing in short events because of their lack of strength and ultimate speed, but are easily competitive in long endurance events. It has been suggested that females are better in the long events such as the marathon because they are capable of metabolizing fat at a greater rate. If true, this would enable the female to spare the use of muscle glycogen. We have attempted to examine this problem and have sampled muscle from male and female runners who possess the same maximal oxygen uptake (61 ml/kg x min), running performances, and who trained at 60-70 miles per week. With these variables held constant we found no differences in fat metabolism of these runners. When asked to run for 1 hour at 70% of their maximal oxygen uptake, both men and women derived 50% of their energy from fat metabolism. Muscle samples taken from these subjects revealed that the males had a significantly greater capacity to metabolize fat than the females and possessed some oxidative enzymes in higher concentrations than the female. Thus it would appear that there is little or no difference between the metabolism and potential performances of males and females who are matched for their aerobic capacities and training backgrounds. Therefore, the differences in performance between the sexes, at the shorter events, may be the difference in muscle strength. This factor is a result of both heredity and sex hormone differences.

SUMMARY

The distance runner is characterized by a variety of anatomical, physiological, and psychological qualities. Although the value of a well-developed cardiovascular system for

36

endurance capacity is well documented in the distance runner, the contractile characteristics and oxidative potential of his running musculature are of equal importance. Several other factors interact to dictate success in distance running. These include sex differences, aging, and variations in body composition. Although early studies identified maximal oxygen uptake (ml/kg x min) as the best single predictor of distance running performance, newer histochemical and biochemical analyses of skeletal muscle appear to offer some potential for improving the accuracy of such predictions. Although our recent research showed few differences between male and female runners, further study is needed to provide a better understanding of the physical qualities that characterize the female distance runner.

REFERENCES

CHAPTER I – REFERENCES,

1. Arstila, M., and Koivikko, A. Electrocardiographic and vectorcardiographic signs of left and right ventricular hypertrophy in endurance athletes. *J. Sports Med. and Phys. Fit.* 6:166-74, 1966.

2. Astrand, P.-O. New records in human power. *Nature.* 176:922-23, 1955.

3. Behnke, A.R., and Royce, J. Body size, shape, and composition of athletes. *J. Sports Med. and Phys. Fit.* 6:75-88, 1966.

4. Boardman, R. World's champions run to types. *J. Hlth. and Phys. Educ.* 4:32 et seq., 1933.

5. Bock, A.V. The circulation of a marathoner. *J. Sports Med. and Phys. Fit.* 3:80-86, 1963.

6. Bowers, R.W., and Costill, D.L. Some physiological characteristics of distance runners. Study presented at the 14th annual meeting, American College of Sports Medicine, 1967.

7. Bramwell, C., Ellis, R. Some observations on the circulatory mechanism in marathon runners. *Quart. J. Med.* 24:329-334, 1931.

8. Comroe, J.H., and others. *The Lung.* Chicago: Yearbook Medical Publishers, Inc., 1963.

9. Consolazio, C.F.; Johnson, R.E.; and Pecora, L.J. *Physiological Measurements of Metabolic Functions in Man.* New York: McGraw-Hill, 1963.

10. Costill, D.L. Metabolic responses during distance running. *J. Appl. Physiol.* 28:251-255, 1970.

11. Costill, D.L. The relationship between selected physiological variables and distance running performance. *J. Sports Med. and Phys. Fit.* 7:61-66, 1967.

12. Costill, D.L., Bowers, R. and Kammer, W.F. Skinfold estimates of body fat among marathon runners. *Med. Sci. Sports.* 2:93-95, 1970.

13. Costill, D.L., Branam, G., Eddy, D. and Sparks, K. Determinants of marathon running success. *Int. Z. Angew. Physiol.* 29:249-254, 1971.

14. Costill, D.L., Daniels, J., Evans, W., Fink, W., Krahenbuhl, G. and Saltin, B. Skeletal muscle enzymes and fiber composition in male and female track athletes. *J. Appl. Physiol.* (In Press).

15. Costill, D.L., Fink, W.J. and Pollock, M. Muscle fiber composition and enzyme activities of elite distance runners. *Med. Sci. Sports.* 8:96-100, 1976.

16. Costill, D.L., and Fox, E.L. Energetics of marathon running. *Med. Sci. Sports.* 7:81-86, 1969.

17. Costill, D.L., Gollnick, P.D., Jansson, E.D., Saltin, B., and Stein, E.M. Glycogen depletion pattern in human muscle fibers during distance running. *Acta physiol. scand.* 89:374-383, 1973.

18. Costill, D.L., Thomason, H. and Roberts, E. Fractional utilization of the aerobic capacity during distance running *Med. Sci. Sports.* 5:248-252, 1973.

19. Costill, D.L. and Winrow, E. Maximal oxygen intake among marathon runners. *Arch. Phys. Med. Rehab.* 51:317-320, 1970.

20. Cureton, T.K. *Physical fitness of champion athletes.* Urbana: University of Illinois Press, 1951.

21. Currens, J.H., and White, P.D. Half a century of running: Clinical, physiological and autopsy findings in the case of Clarence DeMar *New Eng. J. Med.* 265:988-93, 1961.

22. Dill, D.B. Marathoner DeMar: Physiological Studies. *J. Nat. Cancer Inst.* 35:185-191, 1965.

23. Ekblom, B. and Hermansen, L. Cardiac output in athletes. *J. Appl. Physiol.* 25:619-625, 1968.

24. Eriksson, B.O., Gollnick, P.D. and Saltin, B. Muscle metabolism and enzyme activities after training in boys 11 — 13 years old. *Acta physiol. scand.* 87:231-239, 1972.

25. Fox E.L. and Costill, D.L. Estimated cardiorespiratory responses during marathon running. *Arch. Environ. Health.* 24:316-324, 1972.

26. Geddes, D.B. Complete heart block in a distance runner. *Res. Quart.* 27:363-64, 1956.

27. Gibbons, L.W., Cooper, K.H., Martin, R.P. and Pollock, M.L. Medical examination and electrocardiographic analysis of elite distance runners. *Ann. N.Y. Acad. Sci.* 301:283-296, 1977.

28. Gilchrist, A.R. Effect of bodily rest, muscular activity and induced pyrexia on ventricular rate in complete heart block. *Quart. J. Med.* 3:381-99, 1934.

29. Gollnick, P.D., Armstrong, R.B., Saltin, B., Saubert, C.W., Sembrowich, W.L. and Shephard, R.E. Effects of training on enzyme activities and fiber composition of human skeletal muscle. *J. Appl. Physiol.* 34:107-111, 1973.

30. Gollnick, P.D., Armstrong, R.B., Sauberts, C.W., Piehl, K. and Saltin, B. Enzyme activity and fiber composition in skeletal muscle of untrained and trained men. *J. Appl. Physiol.* 33:312-319, 1972.

31. Gorgon, B.; Levine, S.A.; and Wilmaers, A. Observations on a group of marathon runners. *Arch. Intern. Med.* 33:425-34, 1924.

32. Hill, A.V. and H. Lupton. Muscular exercise, lactic acid and the supply and utilization of oxygen. *Quart. J. Med.* 16:135-171, 1923.

33. Hirata, K. Physique and age of Tokyo Olympic champions. *J. Sports Med. and Phys. Fit.* 6:207-221, 1966.

34. Holloszy, J.O. Biochemical adaptations in muscle. *J. Biol. Chem.* 242:2278-2282, 1967.

35. Holmgren, A. and Astrand, P.-O. D_L and the dimensions and functional capacities of the O_2 transport system in humans. *J. Appl. Physiol.* 21:1463-1468,1966.

36. Husman, B.F. Aggression in boxers and wrestlers as measured by projective techniques. *Res. Quart.* 26:421-25, 1955.

37. Kaufmann, D.A., Swenson, E.W., Fencl. J., and Lucas, A. Pulmonary function of marathon runners. *Med. Sci. Sports.* 6:114-117, 1974.

38. Kireilis, R.W. and Cureton, T.K. The relationship of external fat to physical fitness activities and fitness tests. *Res. Quart.* 18:123-34, 1947.

39. Lakie, W.L. Personality characteristics of certain groups of intercollegiate athletes *Res. Quart.* 33:566-73, 1962.

40. Lindsay, J.E., and others. Structural and functional assessments on a champion runner — Peter Snell. *Res. Quart.* 38:355-65, 1967.

41. Montoye, H.J.; Mack, W.; and Cook J. Brachial pulse wave as a measure of cross-country running performance. *Res. Quart.* 31:174-180, 1960.

42. Morgan, W.P. and Costill, D.L. Psychological characteristics of the marathon runner. *J. Sports Med. Phys. Fit.* 12:42-46, 1972.

43. Nason, J., editor. *The Story of the Boston Marathon.* Boston: The Boston Globe, 1966.

44. Pierson, W.R., and Rasch, P.J. Bruce physical fitness index as a predictor of performance in trained distance runners. *Res. Quart.* 31:77-81, 1960.

45. Pollock, M.L., Miller, H. And Wilmore, J. A profile of a champion distance runner: age 60. *Med. Sci. Sports.* 6:118-121, 1974.

46. Pugh, L.G.C.E.; Corbett, J.L.; and Johnson, R.H. Rectal temperatures, weight loss, and sweat rates in marathon running. *J. Appl. Physiol.* 23:347-52, 1967.

47. Raven, P.B., Drinkwater, B.C. and Horvath, S.M. Cardiovascular responses to young female track athletes during exercise. *Med. Sci. Sports.* 4:205-209, 1972.

48. Robinson, S.; Edwards, H.T.; and Dill, D.B. New records in human power. *Sci.* 85:409-10, 1937.

49. Saltin, B. Metabolic fundamentals in exercise. *Med. Sci. Sports.* 5:137-146, 1973.

50. Saltin, B., and Astrand, P.-O. Maximal oxygen uptake in athletes. *J. Apply. Physiol.* 23:347-52, 1967.

51. Smith, W.G.; Cullen, K.J.; and Thorburn, I.O. Electrocardiograms of marathon runners in 1962 Commonwealth games. *Brit. Heart J.* 26:469, 1964.

52. Szerreiks, E. Ein Fall von totalem Herzblock ohne Leistungsminderung bei vollem activen Militardienst. *Deutscher Militararzt.* 1:380, 1936.

53. Westerlund, J.H., and Tuttle, W.W. Relationship between running events in track and reaction time. *Res. Quart.* 2:95-100, 1931.

54. Wilmore, J.H. and Brown, C.H. Physiological profiles of women distance runners *Med. Sci. Sports.* 6:178-181, 1974.

55. Wilmore, J.H., Miller, H. and Pollock, M. Body composition and physiological characteristics of active endurance athletes in their eighth decade of life, *Med. Sci. Sports.* 6:44-48, 1974.

PHYSIOLOGICAL RESPONSE DURING DISTANCE RUNNING

The human body's ability to tolerate and adapt to physical stress is perhaps best demonstrated by the distance runner. In the following discussion we will consider the physiological stresses imposed on the runner during training and competition. Although many athletes appear to meet the anatomical and physiological prerequisites for distance running, only a select group of individuals achieve outstanding success in this most demanding sport. If the coach and athlete hope to make intelligent judgements with respect to training and racing, they must first understand the physical demands placed on the body during competition.

ENERGY EXPENDITURE

The runner's ability to maintain an extremely high rate of energy expenditure for two hours or more is impressively demonstrated by Derek Clayton, whose 2:08:33 marathon performance cost him roughly 2,650 kcal/42 km (12). In order to run at such speeds the marathoner must increase the rate of muscular energy production by more than 15 times the resting level. On the average, distance running requires approximately 60 kcal/km or about 96 kcal/mile. Margaria, *et al.* (51) and others (13,56) have shown that the total energy expenditure of horizontal running per kilometer is constant and independent of velocity. That is to say, running a given distance will require the same amount of energy regardless of the runner's speed. Only the rate of energy utilization will differ. This is illustrated by the regression in Figure 2-1. Using subject Ted Corbitt as an example, we see that to run a marathon at a velocity of 200 meters/min. (eight min/mile) would cost him 11.3 kcal/min. (VO_2 = 2.25 L/min). At that speed it would require 209.6 minutes for him to complete the distance with a total energy expenditure of 2,370 kcal. If he were able to cover the same distance at a speed of 268 meters/min. (six min/mile), requiring 15.9 kcal/min (VO_2 = 3.25 L/min), his running time would be reduced to 157.2 minutes with a total energy expenditure of 2,499 kcal. Although his average velocity was increased 34%, the total energy expenditure increased only 5.4%.

Of course we must not ignore the fact that runners are not equally efficient at all running speeds. This is illustrated by the difference in oxygen requirements for the two middle-aged (45 and 49 years of age) marathoners in Figure 2-1. At all running speeds above 200 m/min., McDonagh uses substantially less oxygen than Corbitt. Since these men had similar aerobic capacities (64-65 ml/kg x min), it is obvious that McDonagh's running efficiency provided him with a decided advantage during their many competitive encounters. This is documented in Table 2-1. It can be seen that although both men used about the same percentage of their aerobic capacities (85%) during marathon races, McDonagh generally averaged about 13:00 faster than Corbitt.

Various studies with sprint, middle distance and distance runners have shown that marathon runners are perhaps more efficient than other trained runners (12,14,15,16,28). In general, they appear to be 5 to 10% more efficient in terms of net oxygen cost per horizontal meter and per kilogram of body weight (ml/kg x min) than middle-distance runners. This advantage, although small for runs of "short" duration, would be an important consideration during the 2 to 3 hours required

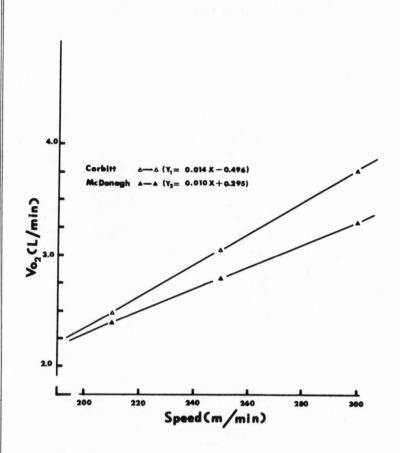

FIGURE 2-1.
OXYGEN REQUIREMENTS DURING RUNNING AT VARIOUS
SPEEDS FOR TWO MIDDLE-AGED MARATHON RUNNERS.

*Runners are not equally efficient. While Corbitt and McDonagh
had similar aerobic capacities, McDonagh was the more efficient,
and therefore, often the faster, runner.*

Table 2-1. Performance data for two middle-aged distance runners (5).

(mon/yr)	Distance (km)	Corbitt Time (hr:min.sec.)	Place	McDonagh Time (hr:min.sec.)	Place
2/67	42.2	2:51.40	8	2:46.21	6
4/67	42.2	2:45.20	81	2:29.55	22
5/67	42.2	2:48.08	11	2:30.06	1
5/67	60.4	4:02.29	4	3:36.52	1
6/67	42.2	3:08.42	14	2:43.42	2
2/68	42.2	2:51.33	8	2:44.40	4
4/68	42.2	2:52.00	43	2:39.34	19
5/68	42.2	2:45.37	6	2:36.35	2
5/68	60.4	4:29.17	3	3:50.11	1
6/68	42.2	3:02.54	10	2:46.51	1
8/68	42.2	2:55.01	8	2:36.36	1
2/69	42.2	2:42.40	9	2:37.25	6
4/69	42.2	2:42.02	56	2:29.07	13
5/69	60.4	3:57.01	2	3:48.11	1
5/69	42.2	2:49.41	5	2:39.34	3

to run a marathon race. It is interesting to note that the net oxygen consumption of world-class middle-distance runners is lower than that of less successful middle-distance runners (51,28,29,46). These differences in running economy can probably be accounted for by the variations in running form required for the two types of events. Film analyses reveal that middle-distance runners have significantly greater vertical displacement when running at speeds from 200 to 325 m/minute than do marathoners (unpublished). Such speeds are well below those required during middle-distance races, and probably do not represent the functional running efficiency of competitors in shorter events (e.g. 800 meters).

Although it is important for the runner to be efficient, we must remember that the upper limits of energy expenditure are restricted by one's *capacity* for oxygen consumption. As discussed in Chapter 1, successful distance runners are characterized by their ability to consume very large volumes of oxygen during exhaustive running (VO_2 max). Such capacities enable the runner to meet the aerobic energy demands of distance competition without heavily taxing the oxygen transport system. If, for example, two runners having VO_2 maximum values of 60 ml/kg x min. (runner A) and 70 ml/kg x min. (runner B) were asked to run at 260 m/minutes, both men would have to consume about 52 ml/kg x minutes. Nevertheless, the demands placed on their aerobic capacities would be markedly different. Runner A would be working at 87% of his VO_2 maximum, whereas runner B would only use 74% of his VO_2 maximum. Subsequently, runner B could probably sustain his pace for a significantly longer time and would theoretically be capable of tolerating prolonged runs at higher speeds than subject A.

The relative energy expenditure (% VO_2 max) for men competing at distances of 5 to 84 km has been estimated from treadmill data (13). As can be seen in Figure 2-2, there is an inverse curvilinear relationship with increasing distance. Although there is some individual variability in the shape of this curve, marathon runners generally require 75 to 80% VO_2 maximum during competition. As pointed our earlier, however, two of the world's best marathoners, Shorter and Clayton, are able to use between 85 to 90% VO_2 maximum during marathon competition. Most runners can tolerate this level of effort only in shorter distances such as a ten-mile (16.1 km) race. As shown in Table 2-2, there are wide variations in % VO_2 maximum that runners are able to use in such races. It should be noted that there is no apparent relationship between the % VO_2 used and either the order of finish or the lactic acid present in the blood following the race.

Since runners seldom maintain a steady pace throughout a race, actual oxygen uptake measurements made during competition are probably more indicative of the peak loads placed on the oxygen transport system during such an effort than they are of the average % VO_2 maximum. In 1973, we measured the oxygen consumption of a competitor during the Lidingoloppet, a 30 km cross country race (17). The data revealed that the % VO_2 maximum varied from 76% during downhill running to 90% during uphill running. During these same intervals heart rates averaged 174 and 180 beats/min. respectively, compared to the subject's maximal heart rate of 189 beats/min.

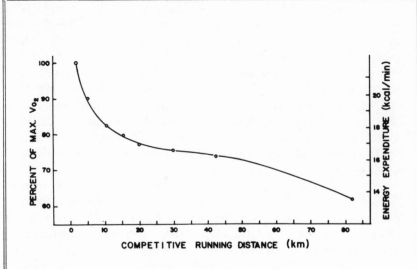

FIGURE 2-2.
PERCENTAGE OF THE RUNNER'S MAXIMAL OXYGEN
UPTAKE UTILIZED DURING COMPETITION
IN RACES OF VARIED DISTANCES.

Most marathon runners require 75 to 80% VO$_2$ maximum during competition. A Frank Shorter or Derek Clayton can use up to 85 to 90% VO$_2$ max during marathon competition, however. Most runners can tolerate this level of effort only for shorter distances, such as 10 miles.

46

Table 2-2. Individual performances and estimated oxygen consumption during a 10-mile race (19).

Subject	10 mile time (min)	Avg Speed (m/min)	Est VO_2* ml/kg/min	% VO_2* max	Post Race L.A.(mM/L)
DBL	48.9	329	72	88	7.0
EH	49.0	328	66	83	9.8
RB	49.1	328	68	90	-----
JB	50.5	318	64	82	6.2
FP	51.6	311	62	90	9.4
DL	51.8	310	63	99	8.0
BS	54.3	296	51	87	7.6
DB	54.6	295	55	83	5.6
DO	55.1	292	61	86	8.0
GE	57.4	280	56	88	-----
MP	59.5	270	52	92	8.6
JF	60.8	265	50	82	7.6
DG	60.8	265	50	81	7.7
BP	63.6	253	50	91	6.2
HP	66.6	242	46	80	8.6
PS	67.8	237	47	84	-----
Mean	56.3	289	51.1	86.1	7.7

*Not corrected for air resistance

Despite the runner's option to reduce pace to compensate for variations in terrain, it is obvious that a hilly course may be more costly than a level one. This is substantiated by several physiological measurements. Gregor (35) has shown that when compared to horizontal running (200 m/min), an incline of 6% (6 meters of vertical lift per 100 meters of horizontal distance) requires 35% more energy. Running down a similar grade, however, only reduced the effort by 24%. Therefore, despite a potential balance between uphill and downhill running, a hilly terrain will significantly impair the runner's performance. Some runners, nevertheless, seem to be considerably more efficient in running up and down various inclines than their competitors. At the speed and grade previously mentioned (200 meters/min $\pm$ 6%), the individual oxygen requirements varied from 50.0 to 60.6 ml/kg x min. on the incline, and from 27.4 to 34.1 ml/kg x min. on the downslope. To confuse the matter even further, there seems to be little relationship between a runner's efficiency during uphill, horizontal, and downhill running. Such information might explain the preference and variations in performance of runners during competition over flat and hilly courses.

Variation in terrain can markedly effect both the mechanics and metabolism of the runner. For example, when runners were asked to run at 70% VO_2 max for 2 hours on varied inclines, it was found that the vastus lateralis muscle (thigh) was metabolically more active during uphill and downhill effort than during level running (18). This would suggest the need for including grade running in training to compensate for these specific demands of road and cross country competition.

Moreover, the energy demands of running are compounded by variations in air-resistance. Studies by Pugh (55) and Hill (39) suggest that during distance running roughly 5 to 8% of the energy spent is needed to overcome air resistance. The energy cost of running at a constant speed but at different wind velocities increased as "head-wind" increased. Pugh (55) has demonstrated that when running on a track in calm air the difference in VO_2 between track and treadmill running will increase with the cube of running velocity. The difference in oxygen consumption can, therefore, be computed by the equation: $VO_2 = 0.002\ V^3$, where VO_2 is in liters/min., and V is the velocity of the air in meters/sec. It is also shown that at the highest running speed (sprinting) with respect to wind resistance, variations in the contour of the trunk, limbs and clothing also affect resistance to movement. These findings demonstrate that a considerable advantage is gained by an athlete who selects to run in the aerodynamic shadow of a competitor.

CIRCULATORY DEMANDS

Since distance running is principally an aerobic task, great demands are placed on the cardiovascular system. During competition its major function of transporting nutrients and wastes is taxed to a maximum. As a measure of this stress, Fox, *et al.* have estimated that marathoners performing a 2:26:30 marathon maintain a cardiac output (Q) of 26.5 liters/min. as compared to their maximal Q of 28.8 1/min. This represents approximately 92% of their maximum cardiac output. At the same time, stroke volume and heart rates averaged 148.6 ml/beat and 178 beats/min., which were also near maximum (153 ml/beat and 188 beats/min., respectively).

We must realize that these average values obtained during prolonged exercise are somewhat misleading. They suggest that Q, stroke volume and heart rates are constant throughout the race. This is certainly not the case. Saltin and Stenberg (68) have shown that during 195 minutes of exercise at 75% VO_2 max, which is similar to the % VO_2 max used in marathon running, Q rose 10% with a 5% increase in oxygen consumption. The major circulatory changes during this exercise bout were the progressive rise in heart rate (15%) and fall in stroke volume (-12%). The causes for these changes are not known. Rowell (63) has speculated that the rise in heart rate and fall in stroke volume are caused by a rise in body temperature with increased distribution of blood flow to the skin (63). When body temperature is elevated, as is the case in distance running, central blood volume and stroke volume fall (64, 65), and Q must be maintained by increasing heart rate (65).

To complicate this picture even more, it should be pointed out that during the initial minutes of running, plasma volume (PV) decreases. Various investigators have shown that this PV change is due to hydrostatic fluid shifts from the intravascular to extravascular compartments (50, 48). The immediate effect of this PV loss is a relative increase in hematocrit and hemoglobin concentrations. In recent studies where we have examined the water content of active and inactive muscles during prolonged exercise, the data confirm that at the onset of exercise water leaves plasma and enters the interstitial space of the working muscle. No change was found in the water content of inactive muscle. Although the consequences of this plasma volume shift and the relative increase in hemoglobin on oxygen transport are not fully understood, we might anticipate an enhanced capacity for oxygen carrying capacity.

Thus the major change in the cardiovascular system under the stress of distance running appears to be a gradual increase in peripheral venous compliance, causing blood volume shifts from the central vasculature to the periphery. Cardiac filling pressure, central blood volume, and stroke volume are reduced so that Q must be maintained by increased cardiac rate. Whether the circulatory transport of oxygen is limited by myocardial fatigue remains unknown. Nevertheless, with exhaustion, sympathetic outflow may increase, causing constriction of capacitance vessels and blood flow to less active regions of the body (skin) (5). This may be responsible for the pallor and gastrointestinal upset sometimes seen at exhaustion.

RESPIRATORY RESPONSES

Associated with the high rate of oxygen consumption during long distance running is the capacity to breathe extremely large volumes of air for extended periods of time (15). This measure is the most obvious, subjective, indicator to help the runner judge his level of stress. Although the volume of air breathed per minute is not a perfect correlate of oxygen consumption, the runner can adjust his running pace to permit a tolerable level of respiratory distress.

While the average man breathes approximately 6 liters of air per minute at rest, Kollias observed volumes in excess of 150 liters per minute during a simulated 5-mile cross-country run. 2-3 illustrates the pulmonary ventilation for three men during a treadmill simulated 10,000-meter run. These runners were able to ventilate between 120 and 145 liters of air per minute for more than 20 minutes of running. Other well trained athletes are found capable of such large pulmonary volumes only during the final stages of an exhaustive run.

One might ask the question, "Does respiratory function limit the capacity for exercise in trained distance runners?" At least two points should be considered in answering this question. First, the work of pulmonary ventilation provides a significant energy demand. The oxygen consumed by the respiratory muscles under resting conditions is only a small fraction (about 1%) of the total body metabolism. With increasing ventilation, the oxygen cost per unit ventilation becomes progressively greater. During distance races where pulmonary ventilation may average 100-120 liters/min., 9 percent of the total energy expenditure may be needed for breathing (53). Since the actual work efficiency of the respiratory muscle cannot be accurately measured, it is impossible to be precise in our estimates of how much energy is needed to ventilate the lungs. In any event, though the work of breathing increases with increased ventilation, it is probably not a limiting factor in long distance running except perhaps at high altitude.

50

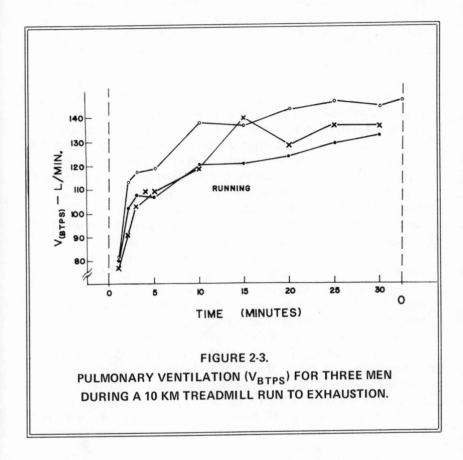

FIGURE 2-3.

PULMONARY VENTILATION (V_{BTPS}) FOR THREE MEN DURING A 10 KM TREADMILL RUN TO EXHAUSTION.

The second consideration in judging the role of respiration as a limitation of endurance performance is the question of maintaining normal blood gases during exercise. Previous studies have demonstrated that arterial oxygen saturation and tension remain fairly constant at different levels of exercise (3). However, in athletes with ventilations of 120 to 150 liters/min., a fall in arterial oxygen saturation has been observed at the end of exhaustive exercise (67, 72). Since long distance runners (e.g., marathoners) seldom tax their respiratory systems to maximum during competition it is unlikely that the pulmonary diffusing capacity will limit their performances. This may not be the case, however, in shorter races (i.e., 5,000 and 10,000 meters). Further studies are needed to determine the effects of such high intensity running on the arterial oxygen saturation during the final stages of such competition. Of course, this will prove valuable only if we can determine the working muscles' ability to use the oxygen delivered to it by the circulation.

All runners attempt to monitor their sensations of effort during distance running in order to judge their pace. Aside from the visual clues of the speed of movement and the sensations of muscular effort, the runner has little to directly indicate the rate of energy expenditure. One of the best indicators of metabolic effort is the direct response of respiratory rate and depth which quickly indicates to the runner his level of effort. It might also be noted that during distance running in warm weather the respiratory responses can usually provide some indication of excessive heat storage. When the runner begins to overheat and the internal body temperature rises, respiration becomes very labored and should be used as a warning.

CHANGES IN BLOOD CONSTITUENTS

Venous blood has long been widely used to describe the physiological responses to exercise, and among its constituents lactic acid has been one of the most studied. Many athletes believe the term "lactic acid" is synonymous with "exhaustion." Even in distance racing there may be a sizeable increase in blood and muscle lactate. During the initial seconds or minutes of a race, the runner's circulatory and respiratory systems are somewhat delayed in their adjustment to the sudden burst of energy. The immediate oxygen requirements are greater than the supply and the runner's muscles must derive their energy in the absence of sufficient oxygen. Thus the runner incurs an oxygen debt and lactic acid accumulates. Although most authorities agree that the accumulation of blood lactic acid gives a good indication of the degree of exhaustion in exercise of short duration, it shows little relationship to exhaustion in distance running competition.

As can be seen in Figure 2-4, blood lactic acid at the end of various distance races is inversely related to the distance. The reason for this is twofold. First, the longer the race, the smaller the % VO_2 max used during running. Consequently, less of the work is done anaerobically and little lactate is produced. Secondly, the lactate produced in the early stages of running may be removed by less active tissues (e.g., liver, kidney, skeletal muscles, etc.), even during exercise (9, 36, 40, 49). It has been shown that the lactic acid produced during an hour of exercise reaches a peak concentration in the blood during the first 10 minutes of running (62). Roughly half of that, however, is removed by the end of 27.5 minutes of exercise. These and other studies (4) strongly suggest that changes in blood lactate and/or tissue pH are seldom, if ever, responsible for the fatigue and exhaustion commonly experienced by the distance runner.

Among the blood's other constituents, it is well known that glucose is one of the primary sources of energy during prolonged endurance exercise. Unless glucose is provided in a drink, blood levels must be maintained by the breakdown of glycogen in the liver. Rowell, *et al.* (61) have shown that the longer the period of exercise, the greater is the glucose output from the liver tissue. Exercising muscles, on the other hand, show a greater uptake and metabolism of blood glucose with exercise duration (74). When the muscle's demands for glucose are greater than the liver's output, however, then blood glucose levels may fall quite low (50 mg/100 ml) because the liver glycogen stores begin to fall. This is often the case in the final stage of a marathon. Venous blood samples obtained from two runners during marathon competition show a gradual decline in glucose concentration (Figure 2-5). Since blood glucose also serves as the principal source of fuel for the nervous system, hypoglycemia may be one factor responsible for exhaustion during distance running.

An alternate source of energy during prolonged endurance exercise is provided by free fatty acids. These shorter-chained fat molecules are released from the fat cells and are transported through the blood to the muscle where they are taken up and metabolized. This fuel provides the rich energy needed for long

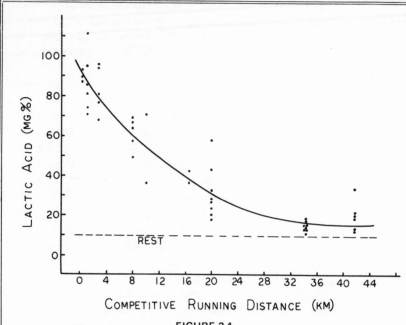

FIGURE 2-4.
BLOOD LACTIC ACID CONCENTRATION AT THE END OF
DISTANCE RACES OF FROM 1.6 TO 42 KM IN LENGTH.

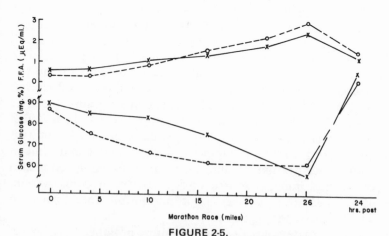

FIGURE 2-5.
BLOOD GLUCOSE AND FREE FATTY ACID
CONCENTRATIONS IN TWO RUNNERS DURING A
MARATHON RACE. SAMPLES OF BLOOD WERE ALSO
MEASURED 24 HOURS AFTER THE COMPETITION.

A Scientific Approach to Distance Running

term running. Unfortunately the processes of breaking down the more complex fat molecules (triglyceride) in fat cells is difficult and has a slow response time. As a result, the runner does not reap the full benefits of fat metabolism until he or she has been running for 30 minutes or longer. This shift toward the use of fat is indicated by a rising level of plasma free fatty acids throughout exercise, and a concomitant increase in plasma glycerol, a by-product of the breakdown of triglyceride. It is important to understand the role of fat metabolism in endurance exercise since it provides an alternate source of energy and spares the premature exhaustion of muscle glycogen stores. Further attention will be given to this topic later in this chapter.

There are obviously other changes in blood constituents during distance running, but none has been discussed as a potential threat to either the runner's performance or health. At this point, however, some mention should be made of the observed changes in serum enzyme concentrations. Following prolonged endurance exercise it is common to observe a large increase in the levels of certain serum enzymes, glutamic oxaloacetic and pyruvic transaminases (GOT and GPT), lactic dehydrogenase (LDH), and creatinine phosphokinase (CPK) (44, 60, 75, 67). Although numerous efforts have been made to link these elevated serum enzymes to tissue damage, no direct evidence is available to substantiate this hypothesis.

It seems equally feasible that these serum enzymes are elevated as a result of leakage from the active tissues. This is compatible with early studies which demonstrate an increased cell membrane permeability following prolonged muscular activity (41). In any event, there seems to be a lack of agreement concerning both the cause and significance of increased serum enzymes following distance running.

As previously discussed, at the onset of running there is a transcapillary fluid flux of water from plasma into the working musculature (50). This loss of water from the blood causes many of the plasma constituents to become concentrated since most do not move out of the vessels as rapidly as water. Subsequently, we may see a marked increase in some plasma particles (e.g., cholesterol, protein, etc.) even though the absolute volume of these items in circulation does not change.

MUSCLE METABOLISM

Laboratory and field studies provide a wealth of information which demonstrate that carbohydrates are the primary source of energy during most types of athletic competition (9, 17, 69). These are supplied by the liver, as blood glucose, and from muscle glycogen stores. At the onset of exercise, muscle glycogen is the primary source of carbohydrate for the muscles. As muscle glycogen stores decline, however, there is an increase in the uptake and utilization of blood-borne glucose. Nevertheless, when muscle glycogen levels are very low, the runner must reduce his speed and exhaustion easily sets in (6, 7, 17, 22).

Figure 2-6 illustrates that the rate of muscle glycogen deflection is dependent on the % of VO_2 max employed during exercise. These data agree with early studies by Christensen and Hansen (11), who showed that at exercise levels below 95% VO_2 max both carbohydrates and fats are used as fuels. Above this work level, however, carbohydrates are used almost exclusively. Total or near total depletion of muscle glycogen is only found if the exercise lasts for more than 50 to 60 minutes at greater than 80% VO_2 max (38, 70).

Although early studies (38) of cycling showed that one hour of exercise (80% VO_2 max) was adequate to deplete the glycogen content of the thigh muscles, a 16.1 km run to exhaustion (roughly 60 minutes) revealed that substantial quantities of glycogen were still available in this muscle (vastus lateralis) after the exercise (22, 38). At first we might be led to think that exhaustion in running is not related to the depletion of muscle glycogen. However, there are two other possible explanations for this discrepancy between muscular exhaustion in cycling and running.

The first contends that the muscle group studied (thigh) was the primary worker during cycling, but did not represent the musculature used during distance running. We, therefore, had men run on a level treadmill for two hours and obtained muscle biopsies from the vastus lateralis, soleus, and gastrocnemius at rest and after 70 and 120 minutes of running (18). Substantially less glycogen was used from the vastus lateralis than the other two muscles, suggesting that the thigh is not a representative muscle group to use in studying exhaustion during running. Only during uphill and downhill running is the

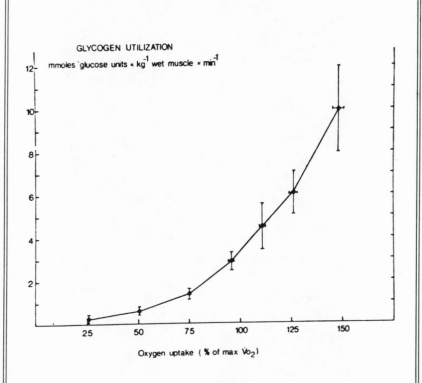

FIGURE 2-6.

RELATIONSHIP BETWEEN MUSCLE GLYCOGEN UTILIZATION AND THE PERCENTAGE OF MAXIMAL OXYGEN UPTAKE USED DURING EXERCISE (FROM SALTIN, *MED. SCI. SPORTS)* **5:137-146, 1973.**

At rates below 95% VO₂ max, both carbohydrates and fats are used as fuels; above this work level, however, carbohydrates are used almost exclusively.

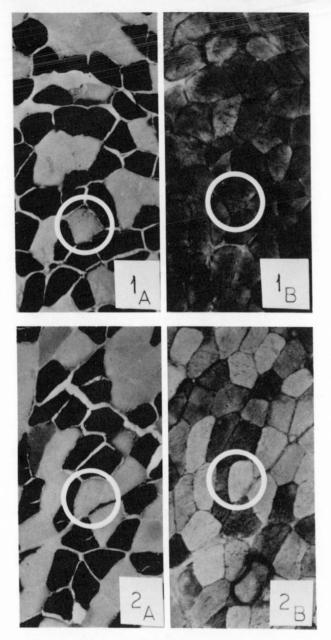

FIGURE 2-7.
MICROSCOPIC EXAMINATION OF GLYCOGEN STORED IN THE SLOW (NO STAIN) AND FAST TWITCH (DARK STAIN) MUSCLE FIBERS BEFORE (1A AND 1B) AND AFTER (2A AND 2B) A 30 KM CROSS-COUNTRY RACE. PHOTOS ON LEFT REPRESENT MYOSIN ATP-ase STAIN FOR FIBER TYPE, WHILE THE PHOTOS ON THE RIGHT ARE STAINED FOR GLYCOGEN CONTENT.

A Scientific Approach to Distance Running

thigh required to metabolize glycogen at rates approximating those of the muscles of the lower leg (18). Even under these circumstances, the muscle glycogen content did not approach zero, despite extreme exhaustion.

Let us consider a second finding that might be used to implicate muscle glycogen depletion as a cause for exhaustion during distance running. Since human muscle contains two types of fibers (slow and fast twitch) it is possible that glycogen might be selectively depleted from some muscle fibers, while remaining only slightly reduced in others. In 1972, we studied the utilization of glycogen in slow (ST) and fast twitch (FT) muscle fibers before and after a 30 km cross-country race (17). Microscopic examination of these muscle samples (Figure 2-7) revealed that the glycogen content of the ST fibers was nearly depleted, while the FT fibers still contained considerable quantities. The fact that ST fibers are metabolically more active during distance running suggests that they are used more extensively in this type of exercise. When these fibers have relinquished their glycogen stores, the FT fibers are apparently unable to generate enough tension to compensate for the exhausted ST fibers. As a result, the runner finds each stride more difficult and finally becomes exhausted when the ST and FT fibers fail to develop sufficient tension. This selective depletion of muscle glycogen is undoubtedly the cause of muscle distress often described by runners during the final stage of marathon competition.

Until now we have discussed only carbohydrate metabolism in distance running. It would be unfortunate to leave the impression that fats and proteins are of minor importance to the endurance performer. To the contrary, both lipids and amino acids have been shown to serve as significant energy sources during long runs. For example, Felig *et al.* (30,31) have demonstrated that alanine is released from exercising muscles and is taken up by the liver. There it serves to produce glucose for the blood. This alanine-glucose cycle, however, probably comes into play only during extremely long runs of 42 km (26.2 miles) or more.

Extra- and intramuscular fat depots, on the other hand, are extensively drawn upon during races longer than 10 km (@ 6.2 miles). Up to that distance, runners use only carbohydrates since they perform at more than 90-95% of their VO_2 max (69). By measuring the respiratory exchange of oxygen and carbon dioxide (R), we can estimate the percentage of energy derived from both lipids and carbohydrates. During a

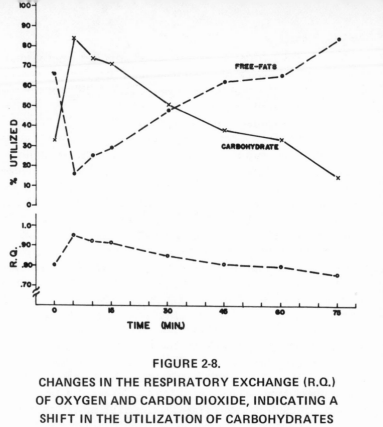

FIGURE 2-8.

CHANGES IN THE RESPIRATORY EXCHANGE (R.Q.)
OF OXYGEN AND CARDON DIOXIDE, INDICATING A
SHIFT IN THE UTILIZATION OF CARBOHYDRATES
AND FATS BY THE WORKING MUSCLES.

2-hour treadmill test (at 65% VO_2 max) we have observed a
decrease in R from 0.88 at 10 minutes of exercise to 0.80 at
120 minutes (Figure 2-8) (15). This indicates that fats
contributed 39% of the total energy for running at 10 min and
67% during the final minutes of exercise. This increased rate of
fat oxidation is the result of increased availability of free fatty
acids (37). Although it is well known that triglycerides are
stored in skeletal muscle, their importance during endurance
effort is not fully understood. Froberg *et al.* support the
concept that they are a major energy source during exercise
(33,34). Regardless of their origin, lipids make a major
contribution to the energy needs of the endurance runner.

A Scientific Approach to Distance Running

THERMOREGULATORY RESPONSES

Probably no single factor poses a greater threat to the distance runner's health and performance than does overheating. With the high rate of energy expenditure, heat production by the working muscles may be 20 times greater than at rest. Attempts by the body to govern heat storage is the responsibility of the hypothalamus, located in the third ventricle of the brain. Functioning as a thermostat, the hypothalamus directs sweating and skin blood flow to facilitate heat loss. Although surprisingly effective, this system of cooling is not without limitations, and often is no match for the high rate of heat production.

One of the primary responsibilities of the circulatory system is to transport the heat generated by the muscles to the surface of the body where it can be transferred to the environment. Since the volume of blood available to carry on the duties of transport (heat, nutrients, waste, etc.) is limited, exercise poses a severe, complex problem for the circulatory system. A large part of the cardiac output must be shared between the skin and working muscles. Thus, any factor that tends to overload the cardiovascular system (e.g. environmental heat) or reduce the transfer of heat to the environment (e.g. high humidity) will drastically impair the distance runner's performance and increase the risk of overheating.

Fink *et al.* (32) have recently demonstrated that exercise in the heat (40°C) places greater demands on muscle glycogen metabolism than during similar work in a cold (9°C) environment. Consequently, a runner attempting to maintain a fast pace during a race on a hot day may experience premature exhaustion due in part to muscle glycogen depletion. This may also explain why some runners recover more slowly from competition in the heat than in the days following a race under cool conditions.

Since runners produce such large amounts of muscle heat, even moderate air temperatures or humidity can result in a critical accumulation of body heat. Pugh, *et al.* (54) and others (24,77) have reported central body temperatures (rectal) greater than 40.0°C (104.0°F) after a marathon race conducted on a moderately warm day. Following a marathon race in the heat (dry bulb 31.1°C, relative humidity 85%, cloud cover 0%), we have recorded the rectal temperature of a nonfinisher at 41.3°C

(106.4°F). Even under cool conditions (dry bulb 9-15.7°C, relative humidity 35-82%), marathoners have recorded rectal temperatures of 40.9°C (105.6°F). Wyndham and Strydom (77) have shown that body temperature during distance running is directly dependent on metabolic rate or gross body weight or both. It would be expected, therefore, that in distance running the heavier men would have higher rectal temperatures than lighter men when running at roughly the same pace.

There is little we can do about environmental heat, but it is obvious that the runner must slow his pace in order to minimize the detrimental effects of a warm sunny day. All runners and race promoters should be able to recognize the symptoms of overheating. Our studies with distance runners have shown that there is a fair relationship between subjective sensations and the runner's body temperature (see Table 2-3). Although we are seldom concerned when we observe rectal temperatures of 39-40°C (102.2-104°F) at the end of prolonged exercise, a runner who has a throbbing pressure in his temples and chills should realize that he is rapidly approaching a stage of potential danger that could prove fatal if he continues to race.

Table 2-3. Correlation of Marathon Runner's Symptoms with Rectal Temperatures

Rectal Temperature	Symptoms
104-105 F	Throbbing pressure in the temples, cold sensation over trunk
105-106 F	Muscular weakness, disorientation and loss of postural equilibrium
Above 106 F	Diminished sweating, loss of consciousness

Recently, the American College of Sports Medicine delivered a position statement on the prevention of heat injuries during distance running (2). The seven major guidelines of this statement are as follows:

1. Distance races (above 16km or 10-miles) should *not* be conducted when the wet bulb temperature/globe temperature* exceeds 28°C (82.4°F).

2. During periods of the year when the daylight dry bulb temperature often exceeds 27°C (80°F), distance races should be conducted before 9:00 a.m. or after 4:00 p.m.

3. It is the responsibility of the race sponsors to provide fluids which contain small amounts of sugar (less than 2.5 g glucose per 100 ml of water) and electrolytes (less than 10 mEq sodium and 5 mEq potassium per liter of solution).

4. Runners should be encouraged to ingest fluids frequently during competition and to consume 400-500 ml (13-17 oz) of fluid 10-15 minutes before competition.

5. Rules prohibiting the administration of fluids during the first 10 kilometers (6.2 miles) of a marathon race should be amended to permit fluid ingestion of frequent intervals along the race course. In light of the high sweat rates and body temperatures during distance running in the heat, race sponsors should provide "water stations" at 3-4 kilometer (2-2.5 mile) intervals for all races of 16 kilometers (10 miles) or more.

6. Runners should be instructed on how to recognize the early-warning symptoms that precede heat injury. Recognition of symptoms, cessation of running, and proper treatment can prevent heat injury. Early warning symptoms include the following: piloerection on chest and upper arms, chilling, throbbing pressure in head, unsteadiness, nausea, and dry skin.

7. Race sponsors should make prior arrangements with medical personnel for the care of cases of heat injury. Responsible and informed personnel should supervise each "feeding station." Organizational personnel should reserve the right to stop runners who exhibit clear signs of heat stroke or heat exhaustion.

*Adapted from Minard, D. Prevention of heat casualties in Marine Corps Recruits, *Milit. Med.* 126:261, 1961.
WB - GT = 0.7 (WBT) + 0.2 (GT) + 0.1 (DBT).

FLUID LOSSES

Dissipation of heat by sweat evaporation results in relatively large body water losses. At the 1968 U.S. Olympic Marathon Trial we observed body weight losses of 6.1 kg (13.4 lb) and estimated sweat rates of 1.09 liters/sq meter/hr (24). The rate of sweating appears to be closely related to the marathoner's average running speed. This point is well documented by Figure 2-9 which illustrates the sweating rates and running speeds of the competitors at the 1968 U.S. Olympic Marathon Trial and 1968 Boston Marathon and provides similar data for 12 marathoners examined in the laboratory.

It is interesting to note that if Derek Clayton were to perform a two-hour, eight-minute, 33-second marathon (327 meters/min. or 20.7 kilocalories/min) under similar meterological conditions, his estimated sweat rate would be about 1.25 liters/sq meter/hr. or a sweat loss of about 5.2 kg. Such sweat losses are large but not uncommon among marathoners.

Despite body weight losses of more than 8%, plasma volume appears to decrease only slightly. Following the initial minutes of exercise, plasma volume only decreases by about 2.0% while the runners' total body weights were reduced by 7.0% (unpublished data). Acute dehydration greater than 2% of body weight is generally believed to decrease plasma volume and significantly impair maximal exercise performance. However, Saltin (71) and Kozlowski *et al.* (46) report little or no decrease in plasma volume after prolonged, severe exercise without fluid replacement. Their findings suggest that a large fraction of the body fluids lost during exercise are drawn from the intracellular spaces. This may explain why marathon runners can tolerate such large sweat losses without experiencing a circulatory collapse.

Wyndham and Strydom (77) have shown that one of the most important factors influencing the level to which the rectal temperature rises during marathon running is the extent of water deficit which the runner allows to develop. When the water deficit exceeds 3% of the man's body weight, even in cool conditions, the runner's rectal temperature will rise. Despite this apparently strong thirst stimulus, runners are generally unable to ingest a sufficient amount of fluid to offset the sweating demands of marathon running.

A Scientific Approach to Distance Running

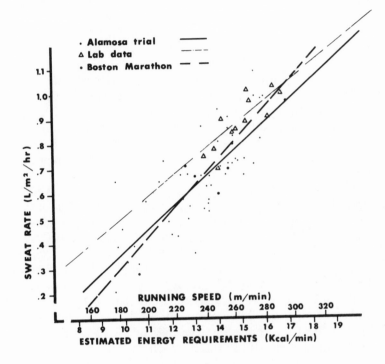

FIGURE 2-9.
RELATIONSHIP BETWEEN RUNNING SPEED (I.E.,
ENERGY EXPENDITURE) AND THE RATE OF SWEATING
DURING MARATHON COMPETITION.

The rate of sweating appears to be closely related to the marathoner's running speed.

FLUID REPLACEMENT

Any factor that inhibits or restricts fluid intake during the early stages of a distance race will promote dehydration and subjects the runner to potential heat injuries. For example, prohibiting the ingestion of fluids during the first 10 km of a marathon may result in a 1.0-1.5 kg. (2.2-3.3 lbs) body water deficit before any fluids can be ingested. While most distance runners strongly support the practice of drinking fluids during competition, there appears to be little consistency with regard to the quantity and composition of the fluids ingested. Observations made during marathon competition demonstrate that despite water deficits of 4 to 6 kg. (8.8 to 13.2 lbs), few runners are able to drink more than 3000 ml (3.1 quarts) of water.

Laboratory measurements demonstrate that marathoners are physically incapable of consuming sufficient amounts of fluids to keep pace with sweat losses (59). During a series of two-hour treadmill runs, marathon runners ingested 100 ml of fluid every five minutes for the first 100 minutes of exercise. Despite the 2 liters (2.1 quarts) of fluid ingested, the men still incurred a 2.0-kg weight deficit. At the end of 100 minutes of running and feeding, it became apparent that further attempts to ingest fluids would have been intolerable. Immediately following the run, approximately 340 ml (0.37 quarts) of the ingested volume was still in the stomach.

However, even partial fluid replacement has been shown to reduce the risk of overheating. Figure 2-10 illustrates the effects of ingesting cold fluids (100 ml each five minutes for 100 minutes) on rectal temperature during two hours of running. When fluids were consumed during the runs, a definite leveling of rectal temperature was observed after about 45 minutes. On the other hand, no thermal balance was seen when fluids were restricted. These laboratory findings are, however, only of theoretical value to the distance runner since the rapid sweat losses, limited rate of gastric emptying, current competitive rules, and feeding habits during the marathon make this practice largely ineffective.

While most solutions ingested during marathon competition contain sugar, to date only limited information is available to describe the effects of glucose feedings during prolonged running. This practice probably stems from reports which indicate that blood glucose levels fall rather drastically

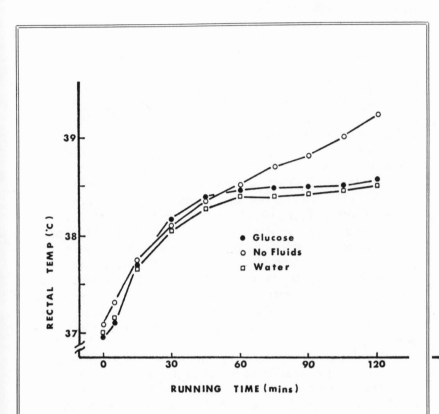

FIGURE 2-10.
CHANGES IN BODY TEMPERATURES DURING
TWO HOURS OF TREADMILL RUNNING,
WITH AND WITHOUT FLUID INGESTION.

during prolonged activity and may reach critically low levels among runners who collapse before finishing the race (10, 59). Costill *et al.* (24) have shown that frequent glucose feeding tends to elevate blood glucose and carbohydrate utilization throughout two hours of exhaustive running.

In the final, often exhaustive, stages of long races, some runners describe a sudden energy lift within minutes following the ingestion of a sugar solution. In theory, this would seem to be compatible with our earlier discussion of hypoglycemia (low blood sugar) during distance races. The intake of sugar might be expected to elevate blood glucose and provide more carbohydrate to vital tissues.

However, we have found that drinking a sugar solution is a relatively slow method of increasing the blood sugar concentration (25). There appears to be a five to seven minute delay from the time the solution is ingested until even traces of the drink appear in the blood. The real physiological benefits of a sugar feeding probably are not realized for 15 to 20 minutes after drinking the solution. We have seen nothing that would explain the almost immediate "lift" reported by the fatigued runner. This is not to say that such feedings do not benefit the runner. To the contrary, although delayed, the sugar that appears in the blood via the intestinal route restores some of the liver's glycogen, thereby lessening the chance of liver glycogen depletion.

A question often raised by runners is, "What is the ideal composition of a solution to be taken during a race?" We have given this problem considerable attention (25, 26, 27), and have concluded that fluid therapy during distance running should conform to the following guidelines:
(1) the drinks should contain less than 2.5 g of glucose per 100 ml water,
(2) contain few, if any, electrolytes; at most 0.2 g sodium chloride,
(3) have an osmolality of approximately 200 mOsm/liter,
(4) be ingested at frequent intervals and in volumes of 100-200 ml,
(5) be cold (40° F or 4° C).

These factors are all important in promoting gastric emptying, for it is of little value to ingest fluid that remains in the stomach. However, even under the most ideal conditions it is unlikely that the maximal rate of gastric emptying (25 ml/min) can match the rate of water lost during heavy sweating

(40-50 ml/min).

From a practical point of view, the runner should realize that carbohydrate and water needs may vary under different conditions. Running on a hot day, for example, the runner may have a greater need for water replacement than for carbohydrate supplementation. On the other hand, cold weather places little demand on water replacement, but the runner might benefit from a sugar feeding. For that reason the composition of the drink administered during prolonged running should be determined on the basis of individual needs and potential benefits.

WARMING UP

The continual controversy concerning the advantages and disadvantages of warming up has been discussed from many angles but remains unresolved (2). Some coaches advocate the importance of warming up for distance on the basis of the following claims:

(1) Warmup increases the muscle temperature and thereby increases the contractile force of the muscle,

(2) Warmup will help to prevent muscle and tendon injuries,

(3) Warmup supposedly brings on second wind more rapidly,

(4) Warmup provides an opportunity to rehearse the pace and relaxation which will be performed during the actual race.

While these potential contributions appear theoretically sound, very little research has been conducted that provides convincing evidence for benefits in distance running. Astrand (4) has reported a five-percent increase in the maximal oxygen uptake capacity of men following a warmup. Since the distance runner's performance relies upon the capacity of his respiratory and circulatory systems to deliver oxygen to the active muscle tissue, such an increase in VO_2 max would be of importance during runs which utilize 100 percent of this capacity. However, races which are performed below this level might not be affected by a lack of warming up. As an example, a miler or two-miler might benefit from warmup while the marathoner might not.

While studying pre- and post-competition rectal

temperatures, Robinson (58) noted a decided detrimental effect of warming up in the heat. Performing a 10,000-meter run in 90°F heat caused the runners to elevate their rectal temperatures approximately 5°F. However, as a result of warming-up, one runner's pre- and post-race rectal temperatures were 1.5°F higher than those of a second runner who did not warmup. It appears quite sensible for the runner to eliminate any warmup prior to a distance race in the heat where one of the major performance limitations is overheating.

While some coaches and researchers feel that warming up is greatly overemphasized, it is apparent that most athletes prefer to continue with traditional techniques. Because of the physiological and psychological complexity of distance running performance, this approach appears to be a wise one.

RACING PACE

Pace is an important but controversial concept. Karpovich (43) suggests that the maximum speed which can be developed depends on the extent to which the metabolism can be raised, and on the efficiency of muscular performance during exercise. However, the oxygen requirements of running increase very rapidly as the velocity of work for the runner becomes greater. Several physiologists have, therefore, advocated an even or steady pace over long distances.

In contrast, Robinson (57) studied the effects of variable pace on the oxygen requirements and blood lactates of four well-conditioned subjects during exhausting treadmill runs. In one experiment, a subject became exhausted in 3.37 minutes while running at a constant speed of 13.9 miles per hour. However, the same runner was able to cover the same distance (1362 yards) in the same total time with a lower oxygen requirement and less blood lactate when he ran the first 2.37 minutes at 13.5 miles per hour and the last minute at 14.9 miles per hour. On the other hand, when the first 2.37 minutes, and last minute were run at 14.9 and 13.5 miles per hour, respectively, the subject experienced higher oxygen requirements and higher blood lactate than while running at the constant speed of 13.9 miles per hour. It must be remembered that such results may be specific to races of relatively short duration.

In a study of heart rate responses to various pace patterns (slow-fast, fast-slow, and steady) during the running of a mile, it was noted that the slow-fast pace pattern required less overall energy than the other pace patterns (8). However, the fast-slow pace pattern was identified as the pattern which produced the fastest one-mile times.

Adams (1) conducted a somewhat more controlled investigation on the energy required to run a 4:37 mile, which was simulated on a treadmill. A steady pace run (Plan 1) consisted of a constant 69.25 seconds per 440-yard pace throughout, while a fast-slow-fast run (Plan 2) involved consecutive 440-yard times of 64, 73, 73, and 67 seconds, and a slow-fast run (Plan 3) required 440-yard times of 71, 71, 67.5, and 67.5 seconds. It was concluded that when the running pace varied from a steady pace, a significantly higher oxygen debt was incurred and that the steady-pace plan was the most efficient means of utilizing one's energy reserves. Hence, the best plan physiologically for accomplishing the fastest time in middle and distance running was the steady-pace strategy.

Additional support for steady pace work was offered by Matthews (52). The mechanical efficiency of exercise was computed while the subjects were riding a bicycle ergometer at 60 revolutions per minute for six minutes with the following distributions of resistance—steady, light-heavy, and heavy-light. His findings indicated that steady pace was significantly more efficient with regard to oxygen consumption.

By means of radio-telemetry, heart rate responses were used by Sorani (73) to elevate steady pace, slow-fast pace, and fast-slow pace during a run of 1320 yards. On the basis of net cardiac cost, no evidence was found that would indicate a detrimental effect caused by varying the pace during a 1320-yard run.

In the light of these research findings, one must conclude that total agreement does not exist relative to the most optimal pace one should employ during a distance race. However, the steady-pace plan appears to have gained the greatest scientific support.

In selecting the best running speed for any given distance race, the coach should remember that the runner is limited by his capacities to consume oxygen and to tolerate fatigue. A series of investigations concerned with the energy expenditure of runners during various distance races has demonstrated a high relationship between the fractional utilization of one's maximal oxygen uptake (VO_2 max) capacity and the length of the race (15). Runners competing in the 2-mile were found to consume

100 percent of their VO_2 max, while 6-milers and marathoners utilized 88-94 percent and 68-75 percent, respectively. Additional research is needed to assess the running speed of champion distance runners as related to their fractional utilization of the VO_2 max. Such information would assist in predicting the potential capacity of a runner to perform at a given distance.

SUMMARY

The preceding discussion has highlighted the responses of the runner's physiology to competition. Although the endurance athlete's physiological capacity is limited by his ability to deliver oxygen to the working muscles, there appear to be marked individual variations in running efficiency and the percentage of the aerobic capacity used during the race. These factors are of major importance in a winning performance.

Several measurements have been identified as responsible for the sensations of fatigue and exhaustion experienced during distance running. These include muscle glycogen depletion, hypoglycemia (low blood sugar), dehydration, and hyperthermia (over-heating). On the other hand, there is little relationship between blood lactic acid concentration and exhaustion during competition.

It has been pointed out, that the runner can obtain some benefits from fluid ingestion during long runs, which may prevent premature exhaustion. Drinks consumed on the run can minimize dehydration, reduce body heat storage and supplement carbohydrate stores. The details of fluid composition and management during the race have been discussed.

REFERENCES

1. Adams, W.C. The effects of selected pace variations on the O_2 requirements of running a 4:37 mile. Proceedings of the National College Physical Education Association for Men, 1966.

2. American College of Sports Medicine. Position statement on prevention of heat injuries during distance running. *Med. Sci. Sports.* 7:7-9, 1975.

3. Asmussen, E. and Nielsen, M. Alveolar-arterial gas exchange at rest and during work at different O_2-tensions. *Acta Physiol. Scand.* 50:153-166, 1960.

4. Astrand, P.O., and others. Blood lactates after prolonged severe exercise. *J. Appl. Physiol.* 18:619-22, 1963.

5. Barger, A.C., Greenwood, DiPalma, J.R., Stoker III, J. and Smith, L.H. Venous pressure and cutaneous reactive hyperemia in exhausting exercise and certain other circulatory stresses. *J. Appl. Physiol.* 2:81-96, 1948.

6. Bergstrom, J. and Hultman, E. A study of the glycogen metabolism during exercise in man. *Scand. J. Clin. Lab. Invest.* 19:218-228, 1967.

7. Bergstrom, J., Hermansson, L., Hultman, E., and Saltin, B. Diet, muscle glycogen and physical performance. *Acta Physiol Scand.* 71:140-150, 1967.

8. Bowles, C.J. Telemetered heart rate responses to pace patterns in the one-mile run. Doctoral thesis. Eugene: University of Oregon, 1965.

9. Carlsten, A., and others. Myocardial metabolism of glucose, lactic acid, amino acids, and fatty acids in healthy human individuals at rest and at different work loads. *Scand. J. Clin. Lab. Invest.* 13:418-28, 1961.

10. Christensen, E.H., Hansen, O. Arbeitsfahigkeit und Ehrnahrung. *Skand Arch Physiol.* 81:160-163, 1939.

11. Christensen, E.H. and Hansen, O. I. Zur Methodik der Respiratorischen Quotient-Bestimmungen in Ruhe und bei Arbeit. II. Untersuchungen uber die Verbrennungsvorgange bei langdauernder, schwerer Muskelarbeit. III. Arbeitsfahigkeit and Ernahrung. *Skand. Arch. Physiol.* 81:137-171, 1939.

12. Costill, D.L., Branam, G., Eddy, D., *et al.* Determinants of marathon running success. *Int Z Angew Physiol.* 29:249-254, 1971.

13. Costill, D.L., Fox, E.L. Energetics of marathon running. *Med. Sci. Sports.* 1:81-86, 1969.

14. Costill, D.L., Winrow, E. A comparison of two middle aged ultra-marathon runners. *Res Quart.* 41:135-139, 1970.

15. Costill, D.L. Metabolic responses during distance running. *J. Appl. Physiol.* 28:251-55, 1970.

16. Costill, D.L., Bowers, R., Branam, G., *et al.* Muscle glycogen utilization during prolonged exercise on successive days. *J. Appl. Physiol.* 31:834-838, 1971.

17. Costill, D.L., Gollnick, P.D., Jansson, E.D., Saltin, B. and Stein, E.M. Glycogen depletion pattern in human muscle fibers during distance running. *Acta Physiol. Scand.* 89:374-383, 1973.

18. Costill, D.L., Jansson, E., Gollnick, P.D. and Saltin, B. Glycogen utilization in leg muscle of men during level and uphill running. *Acta Physiol. Scand.* 91:475-481, 1974.

19. Costill, D.L., Thomason, H. and Roberts, E. Fractional utilization of the aerobic capacity during distance running. *Med. Sci. Sports.* 5:248-252, 1973.

20. Costill, D.L., Cote, R., Fink, W., and Van Handel, P.J. Water and electrolyte changes in active and inactive muscle during prolonged exercise. (Unpublished).

21. Costill, D.L. Muscular exhaustion during distance running. *Physician and Sportsmedicine.* Oct. 1974.

22. Costill, D.L., Sparks, K.E., Gregor, R. and Turner, C. Muscle glycogen utilization during exhaustion running. *J. Appl. Physiol.* 31:353-356, 1971.

23. Costill, D.L., Bowers, R., Branam, G. *et al.* Muscle glycogen utilization during prolonged exercise on successive days. *J. Appl. Physiol.* 31(6):834-838, 1971.

24. Costill, D.L., Kammer, W.F., Fisher, A. Fluid ingestion during distance running. *Arch Environ. Health.* 21:520-525, 1970.

25. Costill, D.L., Bennett, A., Branam, G., *et al.* Glucose ingestion at rest and during prolonged exercise. *J. Appl. Physiol.* 34(6):764-769, 1973.

26. Costill, D.L., Saltin, B. Factors limiting gastric emptying at rest and during prolonged severe exercise. *Acta Physiol Scand.* 71:129-139, 1967.

27. Costill, D.L., Sparks, K.E. Rapid fluid replacement following thermal dehydration. *J. Appl. Physiol.* 34(3):299-303, 1973.

28. Daniels, J., Oldridge, N. The effects of alternate exposure to altitude and sea level on world-class middle-distance runners. *Med. Sci. Sports.* 2:107-112, 1970.

29. Dill, D.B. Oxygen used in horizontal and grade walking and running on the treadmill. *J. Appl. Physiol.* 20:19-22, 1965.

30. Felig, P. and J. Wahren. Amino acid metabolism in exercising man. *J. Clin. Invest.* 50:1702-1711, 1971.

31. Felig. P., T. Pozefsky, E. Morliss, and G.F. Cahill. Alanine; Key role in gluconeogenesis. *Science.* 167:1003-1004, 1960.

32. Fink, W., Costill, D.L. and Van Handel, P.J. Leg muscle metabolism during exercise in the heat and cold. *European J. Appl. Physiol.* 34:183-190, 1975.

33. Froberg, S.O., L.A. Carlsson, and L.-G. Ekelund. Local lipid stores and exercise. *Muscle Metabolism During Exercise* eds. Pernow and Saltin. Plenum Press. 11:307-313, 1971.

34. Froberg, S.O. and F. Mossfeldt. Effect of prolonged strenuous exercise on the concentration of triglycerides, phospholipids and glycogen in muscle of man. *Acta Physiol. Scand.* 82:167-171, 1971.

35. Gregor, R., A comparison of the energy expenditure during positive and negative grade running, Master's thesis, Muncie, Ind., Ball State University, 1970.

36. Harris, P.M., and others. The regional metabolism of lactate and pyruvate during exercise in patients with rheumatic heart disease. *Clin. Sci.* 23:545-60, 1962.

37. Havel, R.J. Influence of intensity and duration of exercise on supply and use of fuels. *Muscle Metabolism During Exercise,* eds. B. Pernow and B. Saltin. Plenum Press. 11:315-325, 1971.

38. Hermansen, L., Hultman, E. and Saltin, B. Muscle glycogen during prolonged severe exercise. *Acta Physiol. Scand.* 71:129-139, 1967.

39. Hill, A.V. The air resistance of a runner. *Proc. Roy Soc London.* 102:380-385, 1928.

40. Himwick, H.E., Koskoff, Y.D., and Nahum, L.H. Studies in carbohydrate metabolism. I.A., glucose-lactic acid cycle involving muscle and liver. *J. Biol. Chem.* 85:571-84, 1930.

41. Holloszy, J.O. and Narahara, H.T. Enhanced permeability of sugar associated with muscle contraction. Studies of the role of Ca++. *J. Gen. Physiol.* 50:551-557, 1967.

42. Jensen, C.R. The controversy of warmup. *Athletic J.* 4:25, 1966.

43. Karpovich. P.V. *Physiology of muscular activity.* Philadelphia: W.B. Saunders, 1965, pp. 1-278.

44. Kew, M.C., Bersohn, I., Seftel, H.C. and Kent, G. Liver damage in heat stroke. *Am. J. Med.* 49:192-202, 1970.

45. Kollias, J., Moody, D.L., and Buskirk, E.R. Cross-country running: Treadmill simulation and suggested effectiveness of supplemental treadmill training. *J. Sports Med and Phys. Fit.* 7:148-54, 1967.

46. Kollias, J., Moody, D.L., Buskirk, E.R. Cross-country running: Treadmill simulation and suggested effectiveness of supplemental treadmill training. *J. Sports Med.* 7:148-154, 1967.

47. Kozlowski, D., Saltin, B. Effect of sweat loss on body fluids. *J. Appl. Physiol.* 19:1119-1124, 1964.

A Scientific Approach to Distance Running

48. Leithead, C.S. and Lind, A.R. *Heat Stress and Heat Disorders.* Philadelphia, PA, F.A. Davis Company, 1964.

49. Levy, M.N. Uptake of lactate and pyruvate by intact kidney of the dog. *Amer. J. Physiol.* 202:302-308, 1962.

50. Lundvall, J. Tissue hyperosmolality as a mediator of vasodilatation and transcapillary fluid flux in exercise skeletal muscle. *Acta Physiol. Scand.* Suppl. 397:1-142, 1972.

51. Margaria, R., Cerretelli, P., Aghems, P. Energy cost of running. *J. Appl. Physiol.* 18:367-370, 1963.

52. Mathews, D.K., and others. Aerobic and anaerobic work efficiency. *Res. Quart.* 34:393-97, 1963.

53. Nielsen, M. Die Respirationsarbeit bei Korperruhe und bei Muskelarbeit. *Skand. Arch. Physiol.* 74:299-316, 1936.

54. Pugh, L.G.C., Corbett, J.I. and Johnson, R.H. Rectal temperature, weight losses, and sweat rates in marathon runnning. *J. Appl. Physiol.* 23:347-352, 1967.

55. Pugh, L.G.C. Oxygen uptake in track and treadmill running with observations on the effect of air resistance. *J. Physiol.* 207:823-835, 1970.

56. Pugh, L.G.C., Corbett, J.L., Johnson, R.H. Rectal temperatures, weight losses, and sweat rates in marathon running. *J. Appl. Physiol.* 23:347-352, 1967.

57. Robinson, S., and others. Influence of fatigue on the efficiency of men during exhausting runs. *J. Appl. Physiol.* 12:197-201, 1958.

58. Robinson, S. Temperature regulation in exercise. *Pediat.* 32, Supplement: 691-702, 1963.

59. Rodahl, K., Miller, H.I., Issekutz, B., Jr. Plasma free fatty acids in exercise. *J. Appl. Physiol.* 19:489-495, 1964.

60. Rose, K.I., Bousser, J.E. and Cooper, K.H. Serum enzymes after marathon running. *J. Appl. Physiol.* 29:355-357, 1970.

61. Rowell, L.R., Masoro, E.J. and Spencer, M.J. Splanchnic metabolism in exercising man. *J. Appl. Physiol.* 20:1032-1037, 1965.

62. Rowell, L.B., and others. Splanchnic removal of lactate and pyruvate during prolonged exercise in man. *J. Appl. Physiol.* 21:1773-83, 1966.

63. Rowell, L.B., Circulation. *Med. Sci. Sports.* 1:15-22, 1969.

64. Rowell, L.B., Marx, H.J., Bruce, R.A., Conn, R.D. and Kusumi, F. Reductions in cardiac output, central blood volume with thermal stress in normal men during exercise. *J. Clin Invest.* 45:1801-1816, 1966.

65. Rowell, L.B., Murray, J.A., Brengelmann, G.L. and Kranning II, K.K. Human cardiovascular adjustments to rapid changes in skin temperature during exercise. *Circulat. Res.* (In Press).

66. Rowell, L.B., Kraning, K.K., Kennedy, J.W. and Evans, T.O. Central circulatory responses to work in dry heat before and after acclimitization. *J. Appl. Physiol.* 22:509-518, 1967.

67. Rowell, L.B., Taylor, H.L., Wang, Y. and Carlson, W.S. Saturation of arterial blood with oxygen during maximal exercise. *J. Appl. Physiol.* 19:284-286, 1964.

68. Saltin, B. and Stenberg, J. Circulatory responses to prolonged severe exercise. *J. Appl. Physiol.* 19:833-838, 1964.

69. Saltin, B. Metabolic fundamentals in exercise. *Med. Sci. Sports.* 5:137-146, 1973.

70. Saltin, B. and J. Karlsson. Muscle glycogen utilization during work of different intensities. *Muscle Metabolism During Exercise.* eds. B. Pernow and B. Saltin. Plenum Press, 11:289-300, 1971.

71. Saltin, B. Aerobic work capacity and circulation at exercise in man: With special reference to the effect of prolonged exercise and/or heat exposure. *Acta Physiol Scand.* 62 (suppl 230):1-52, 1964.

72. Shephard, R.H. Effect of pulmonary diffusing capacity on exercise tolerance. *J. Appl. Physiol.* 12:487-488, 1958.

73. Sorani, R. The effect of three different pace plans on the cardiac cost of 1320-yard runs. Doctoral dissertation. Los Angeles: University of Southern Caifornia, 1967.

74. Wahren, J., Felig, P., Hendler, R. and Ahlborg, G. Glucose and amino acid metabolism during recovery after exercise. *J. Appl. Physiol.* 34:838-845, 1973.

75. Wyndham, C.H., Kew, M.C., Kok, R., Bersohn, I. and Strydom, N.B. Serum enzyme changes in unacclimatized and acclimatized men under severe heat stress. *J. Appl. Physiol.* 37:695-698, 1974.

76. Wyndham, C.H. A survey of research initiated by Chamber of Mines into clinical aspects of heat stroke. Proc. Mine Med. Officer's Assoc. (S. Africa) 46:68-80, 1966.

77. Wyndham, C.H., Strydom, N.B. The danger of an inadequate water intake during marathon running. *S. Afr. Med. J. 43:893-896, 1969.*

ADAPTATIONS TO ENDURANCE TRAINING

Physiological adjustments which compensate for the stresses of endurance training are varied and often specific to the activities employed during training. In light of the demands placed on the runner's physiology during competition (see Chapter 2), it seems appropriate to design the training program in such a way that all essential systems (e.g., circulation) are given ample opportunity for adaptation. First, let us consider the adaptations that occur with endurance training. Our discussion will be limited to the changes in oxygen transport (aerobic capacity and central circulation) and the oxidative potential of the running musculature.

OXYGEN TRANSPORT

Early studies by Saltin *et al.* (76) have shown few changes in respiratory function as a result of endurance training. They observed only an increased diffusing capacity of the lungs, and this was related to an increase in cardiac output with training. An important feature of the gas transport from the lungs to the blood is the alveolar-arterial (A-a) oxygen gradient. Following training, a lower A-a gradient was observed at all levels of exercise, indicating a better ventilation-perfusion ratio.

Several investigators have shown a strong relationship between maximal oxygen uptake (VO_2 max) and red cell mass (5, 41, 80). Some, however, have reported conflicting results on the effects of training on cell mass and total circulating hemoglobin (49, 50, 81). Nevertheless, it is generally agreed that years of training probably increase the red cell mass without changing the hemoglobin content of the cell. Physical conditioning is also shown to have a significant effect on plasma volume (14, 76, 84). While three weeks of bed rest may produce a 15% decrease in plasma volume, one week of activity is sufficient to return it to the prebed-rest value (14). Subsequent endurance training will elevate the plasma volume an additional 10-15%.

Without some increase in red cell mass there may be a marked hemodilution. This may account for the low hematocrit and hemoglobin values often observed during periods of intense training on repeated days (17). Although no convincing evidence is available, we cannot exclude the possibility that during prolonged running the red cell mass may even decrease as a result of red cell destruction. Regardless of these fluctuations in red cell mass and plasma volume, it is generally conceded that total blood volume increases with training. Whether these changes are of significant magnitude to enhance oxygen transport remains equivocal.

Recently some attention has been given to the advantages of blood reinfusion, referred to in the press as "blood doping." In theory, the addition of red blood cells to circulation might be expected to increase the oxygen-carrying capacity of blood, thereby improving the aerobic capacity (VO_2 max). Ekblom *et al.* (31) observed that VO_2 max decreased by 13-18% when 400-800 ml of blood was withdrawn from training subjects. After reinfusion, 4 weeks later, physical performance capacity and VO_2 max increased 23% and 9%, respectively. Although Williams, *et al.* (86) have failed to find an enhancement in endurance performance with blood reinfusion, recent studies (13, 67) support Ekblom's original findings.

One important factor that should be considered when adding larger volumes of red cells to the blood is their effect on blood viscosity. This would increase the resistance to blood flow and in effect would reduce the oxygen transport capacity.

It seems that additional information is needed to permit a full understanding of the hemodynamics of oxygen transport and the role red cell mass plays in physical endurance performance.

Endurance training apparently has little effect on cardiac output during submaximal exercise (12, 73). The striking reduction in heart rate, when working at a given submaximal running speed, is attributed to an increase in stroke volume with training (12, 30, 73). An enhanced capacity to consume oxygen during maximal exercise is the result of increases in maximal cardiac output and arterialvenous oxygen difference. Since maximal heart rate is unchanged or slightly lower after training, the increase in maximal cardiac output is attributed to the increase in stroke volume. With years of training maximal heart rate remains quite constant, but maximal stroke volume may show a marked increase (6). For that reason, Saltin (75) has suggested that stroke volume is the factor that distinguishes the champion endurance athlete from the well-trained individual. The increased stroke volume following training is, in part, achieved by an increase in heart volume (76). We measured the heart volume for Steve Prefontaine to be 1205 ml, which is roughly 30-40% larger than the predicted value for an inactive man of equal age, height, and weight.

Despite some evidence that suggests an increase in the density of muscle capillaries with training, apparently there is no change in muscle blood flow during a given submaximal exercise bout as a result of training (40, 62, 76, 77). During maximal exercise, however, training induces a significant increase in blood distribution to active muscles (76).

Thus with endurance training we see a variety of adaptations which facilitate oxygen transport to the working muscles. The end result is that greater volumes of oxygen can be delivered to the muscle cell. This serves little purpose, however, unless the muscle has developed an enhanced capacity to use greater volumes of oxygen. Therefore, let us consider the training adaptations in skeletal muscle that could promote oxidative energy production during prolonged running.

MUSCULAR ADAPTATIONS

In Chapter 2 some mention was made that during endurance running there is a selective depletion of glycogen from slow twitch (ST) fibers. This suggests that these fibers are metabolically more active and are responsible for generating a major fraction of the tension needed for running. If we assume that the ST fibers are more extensively used during distance running, then it seems likely that the metabolic adaptations to endurance training might also be greatest in the ST fibers. This concept is important when we design a training program that will elicit the specific needs of the muscle fibers that will be used during competition. Later in the chapter additional attention will be given to the specificity of training adaptations in ST and FT fibers.

How does the muscle fiber increase its capacity to perform oxidative metabolism? The cellular structure responsible for this means of energy production is the mitochondrion, often referred to as the "powerhouse" of the cell (Figure 3-1). Therefore, we might expect an increase in the oxidative potential of the cell if training increased either the number of mitochondria per cell or the efficiency of each mitochondrion or both. There is evidence to support both quantitative and qualitative changes in muscle mitochondria with training (39).

The task of breaking down fuels for the production of ATP (adenosine triphosphate), the immediate source of energy for cellular function, is facilitated by specialized proteins, enzymes, located within and outside the mitochondria. As a result of endurance training, there are marked increases in mitochondrial enzyme activities (32, 36, 43, 44). At the same time, training by long endurance running has no effect on the ability of the muscle to form ATP by anaerobic mechanisms (61). This is seen in the fact that succinic dehydrogenase (SDH), a mitochondrial enzyme, may be 3.5 times greater in trained distance runners than in untrained men (18, 19). On the other hand, phosphorylase activity, a rate limiting step in glycolysis, is similar in both untrained and endurance trained runners. That is not to say that training cannot increase the enzymes of glycolysis or improve the capacity for anaerobic exercise. Current evidence suggests that this system of energy production can only be enhanced by high intensity exercise of short duration, such as repeated bouts of sprint running (74, 78).

Training by long continuous running has been shown to increase the oxidative potential of both the ST and FT fibers (36). This is apparently achieved by taxing both fiber types, a condition often met in extremely long training runs. As previously mentioned, the ST fibers are preferentially recruited during the early stages of running, but as they begin to fatigue the FT fibers are employed to compensate for any loss in

80

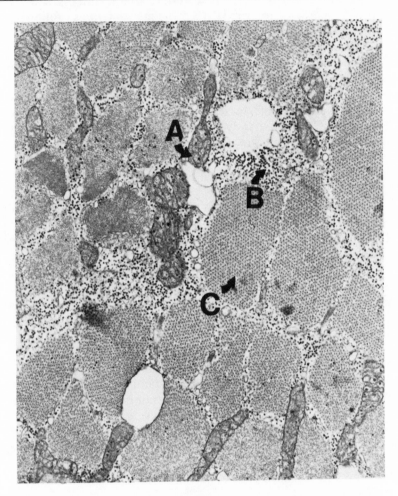

FIGURE 3-1.
ELECTROMICROGRAPH (X 250,000) OF HUMAN
SKELETAL MUSCLE SHOWING THE PRESENCE OF
MITOCHONDRIA (A), GLYCOGEN GRANULES (B), AND
CONTRACTILE FILAMENTS (C) IN A SINGLE FIBER (CELL).

There is evidence that training causes changes in both the quantitative and qualitative aspects of the mitochondria.

muscle tension (21, 37). As a result, the FT fibers show a marked increase in oxidative enzyme activities following endurance training.

With endurance training, then, we see improvements in both the ability of the cardiovascular system to deliver oxygen to the running musculature and an enhanced capacity of the muscle fibers to use the oxygen. The net result is that the trained runner is able to derive larger amounts of energy for sustained muscular effort. At this point one might pose the question, "How much training is needed to achieve these circulatory and cellular adaptations?" Unfortunately, insufficient research has been done to provide us with the answer to this question. Although a variety of studies have been conducted to define the training frequency, duration, and intensity needed for optimal improvement in aerobic capacity, the findings are inconclusive and the research designs often open to criticism (34, 56, 59, 87). One major difficulty in most training studies rests on individual variations in response to a given training stimulus. Unless very large groups of subjects are studied, the effects of various training schedules can be obscured by individual differences in the degree of adaptation to training.

As a result we are again confronted with the fact that not all runners are alike, either in their innate physiology or their capacity to adapt to endurance training. It is unlikely, therefore, that we can design a single training program that will satisfactorily meet the needs of every distance runner. Nevertheless, there are some general guidelines that can be of value in establishing a training schedule for all runners. The following discussion will attempt to compare various forms of training and establish general principles for training the distance runner.

TRAINING INTENSITY

In general, distance training can be categorized as either "long slow distance" (LSD) or "high intensity" running. Of course, there are numerous variations within each category, but the major differences are in the duration and intensity of the runner's effort. First, let us evaluate the advantages and disadvantages of each system as a stimulus for optimal training gains.

Long slow distance running usually involves training at

distances greater than those of actual competition and are performed considerably slower than racing pace. The major advantage of this training system is that it permits the runner to perform a greater amount of work output without subjecting the body to the stresses of high intensity effort. As pointed out earlier, total work output alone may serve as the sole stimulus for aerobic development. For this reason, it is not surprising that many runners who use this system of training have very high VO_2 max values (20, 23).

There are, however, some serious limitations to this type of training when it serves as the only form of stress for the distance runner. First, it fails to develop the neurological patterns of muscle fiber recruitment that will be employed during races which require relatively higher speeds. Secondly, the selective recruitment of muscle fibers may differ at varying running speeds. Thus, during competition some muscle fibers may not be prepared to meet the high rate of energy demands imposed by the faster running speeds. Subsequently, the runner's racing speed may be relatively slow. We have observed that men who use only the LSD method of training seem to show marked improvements in performance when they race frequently. This suggests that the faster speeds of competition serve to supplement the runner's aerobic endurance with patterns of movement that make his efforts more efficient.

High intensity training may include either intermittent running (intervals) or continuous running at near racing pace. Usually the intermittent training bouts are 60 seconds to 5 minutes in duration and are performed at speeds equal to or greater than racing pace. High intensity continuous running can involve training runs of 5 to 10 miles and are generally executed at speeds slightly less than those used during competition over the same distances.

Because high intensity training places greater demands on carbohydrate metabolism, muscle glycogen depletion will prevent a runner from doing a large volume of work. A second disadvantage of this type of training is that it subjects the runner to greater joint and muscle stress and increases the potential for stress injuries (e.g., tenosynovitis) (56). Since the runner is likely to perform less external work by this method of training, one might think that the gains in VO_2 max will not be as great as with LSD training. There is little evidence to support this concept, however (77). To the contrary, several studies (48, 57, 58) have shown that high intensity training programs significantly increase the oxidative capacity of skeletal muscle, while a lower intensity, long-distance program showed no significant increases in the aerobic potential of skeletal muscle (34, 38).

The primary advantage of the high intensity type of training is that it more accurately simulates the rate of energy expenditure and muscle fiber recruitment required during competition. As a result, the adaptations of both the oxygen transport and muscular systems are matched to the task of optimal distance running performance. From the preceding discussion, it becomes obvious that the distance runner might benefit most from a training program containing both LSD and high intensity running.

Since most distance races require a limited capacity for anaerobic metabolism, it seems logical that some high intensity exercise should be included in the training program to stress this system. Since runners who train solely by LSD seem to show significant improvements in performance as a result of a single bout of high intensity exercise (competition), we are led to speculate that the distance runner's training should include one or two high intensity workouts per week.

TRAINING DURATION AND FREQUENCY

Improvements in distance running performance in recent years can, in part, be attributed to changes in training procedures. This is most noticeable when we consider the great distances covered by current runners during training. On the average, elite U.S. distance runners run 160 to 240 km (100 to 150 miles) per week in training (19). This is in contrast to some elite runners of an earlier era. Shrubb, who in 1904 ran 50:55 and 9:17.8 for ten and two miles, respectively, and George, who in 1886 ran the mile in 4:12.8 seconds, both trained on programs that would seem like a warmup by present day standards (79). During his most strenuous training, Shrubb covered 35 miles of moderate running in a 7-day period. In 1882, George (79) reported that he ran fewer than 10 miles (16.1 km) per week, most of it at slow pace. Both men, however, were reported to have trained twice daily and occasionally used sprints with rest intervals between each.

It appears safe to say that few world-class distance runners train at fewer than 70-80 miles per week. A survey (55) of the

125 entries of the 1962 Western Hemisphere Marathon revealed that 60 percent of the runners trained 45-52 weeks per year. Forty-five percent of the participants trained twice each day, and nearly 40 percent ran more than 100 miles per week. As would be expected, those who finished among the leaders employed all of these training procedures (year-around, twice per day, and mileage in excess of 100 miles/week).

Most attempts to evaluate the importance of training frequency on endurance capacity have been limited to studies using previously sedentary subjects (9, 64, 65). Bartels (9) and Pollock *et al.* (65) have shown significant improvements in VO_2 max with 2 and 4 exercise bouts per week, but after 7-13 weeks of training no differences were found between the 2- and 4-day per week training groups. However, after 20 weeks of training the men who trained 4 days per week showed significantly greater gains in VO_2 max (65). It is difficult to extrapolate from these data the training needs of distance runners. We can only judge from current training methods which suggest that only with 5 or 6 training days per week can a runner perform sufficient work to enable him/her to achieve maximal benefits.

It is a fairly common practice for distance runners to train two sessions per day. This method of dividing the total daily training distance into two sessions apparently enables the runner to tolerate a greater volume of running. At present we have no evidence to support or refute this practice. Rogan (70), however, has examined the benefits of supplementing a single daily training session with an early morning distance run (8 km/run). He found no greater improvements in either laboratory (VO_2 max, etc.) or performance (times for 800 meters and 1 mile) measurements for the groups that trained once and twice per day. As with most training studies, there were wide individual variations which might have obscured any true effects of training twice per day.

This does, however, bring up the question, "How much running is necessary for a maximal training effect?" If a runner is currently running 160 km (100 miles) per week, will his performance improve significantly if he increases the training distance to 320 km (200 miles) per week? No information is available to answer that question. It seems only logical that there must be a point at which the volume of work performed will not produce significant gains in performance. One of the factors that seems to limit the runner's capacity for work in training is that of nutrition. With an extremely strenuous training schedule, the runner may experience a state of chronic exhaustion, which seems to be related to muscle glycogen depletion.

DIETARY REQUIREMENTS

Repeated days of intense training have been shown to reduce drastically the glycogen storage in the running musculature (15). After 2 or 3 days of distance running (10 miles/day), muscle glycogen was reduced to near zero (Figure 3-2). A diet containing roughly 50-55% carbohydrate was found to be inadequate in restoring the muscle glycogen to its pretraining level. It has also been shown that some individuals may not restore their glycogen despite 5 days of rest and carbohydrate ingestion (15).

More recently, Piehl (63) has shown that following prolonged exhaustive exercise young men require approximately 46 hours to restore their muscle glycogen to the pre-exercise level. This was in spite of the fact that the subjects were eating a diet high in carbohydrates, 90% of the diet.

Bergstrom and Hultman (11, 46) have studied this problem of glycogen depletion and post-exercise diets. As a result of their efforts, we now know that the muscle glycogen content can be increased well above the normal levels by first emptying the glycogen stores through strenuous exercise and then ingesting a high carbohydrate diet for 3 days. The resulting benefit of glycogen replenishment is localized to the muscles that have been exercised and is referred to as "muscle glycogen supercompensation." A fat-protein diet following exercise, on the other hand, produces a slow, incomplete replacement of glycogen in the exhausted muscles. If carbohydrate is given without previous exercise, only a mild increase in glycogen may occur.

What then is the benefit of this muscle glycogen supercompensation? Based on the discussion in Chapter 2, it becomes obvious that with large muscle glycogen stores, there is significantly less chance of premature exhaustion during races lasting an hour or more. Bergstrom and Hultman have shown that the exercise time to exhaustion can be increased by more than 100 percent as a result of muscle glycogen supercompensation.

Some principles to govern the use of this glycogen storing procedure are: (1) the muscles are most receptive to glycogen

86

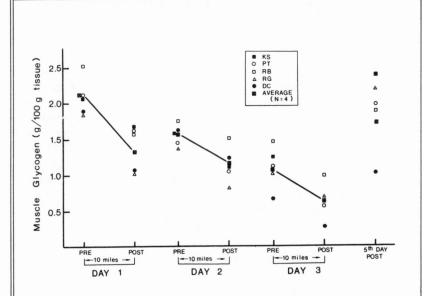

FIGURE 3-2.

**EFFECTS OF THREE REPEATED DAYS OF DISTANCE
RUNNING ON THE GLYCOGEN CONTENT
IN THE LEG MUSCLE (VASTUS LATERALIS).**

*After reducing muscle glycogen to near zero, even a diet
containing roughly 50-55% carbohydrate was found to be
inadequate for restoring glycogen pretraining levels. Some
individuals may not restore their glycogen despite 5 days of rest
and carbohydrate ingestion after total depletion.*

synthesis during the first 10 hours following exhaustive exercise, so the first meal after an exhaustive training run should be high in carbohydrates (e.g., bread, spaghetti); (2) the mean time required to achieve maximal glycogen storage is 3 days; (3) the high carbohydrate diet must be preceded by an exhaustive workout, such as a hard 60 minute run followed by 6-10 fast 400 meter runs; (4) little or no running should be performed in the 3 days of glycogen storing; and (5) all runners do not store glycogen at the same rate nor to the same extent.

Thus far we have only considered the importance of maintaining muscle glycogen for optimal performance. Certainly the liver's contribution of glucose during long runs depends on its glycogen stores. Hultman and Nilsson (47) have presented data which suggest that one hour of heavy exercise will reduce the liver glycogen concentration by 24 g/kg of liver tissue. This would constitute a loss of nearly 60% of the normal liver glycogen stores. Fortunately, the liver can restore such loss with one or two meals containing 50-100 grams of carbohydrate (normal daily carbohydrate intake is 300-400 g). Such information indicates that carbohydrate feedings during or soon after a distance race will rapidly restore liver glycogen, but will have less influence on muscle glycogen resynthesis. Earlier we discussed the value of carbohydrate ingestion during competition (Chapter 2).

Considering the time course for glycogen synthesis (muscle and liver) and the relatively slow rate of digestion, the precompetition meal probably contributes little to the energy needs of the race. On the other hand, a light meal (500 k calories) has no detrimental effect on endurance performance when taken 30 minutes, 1 hour, and 2 hours before running 1-2 miles (3, 4, 85). Larger meals, however, may interfere with respiration and place excessive stress on circulation unless eaten 3 or more hours before competition.

Vitamin supplementation is a common practice among athletes seeking to improve their performance. Although it is known that selected vitamin deficiencies can impair physical performance, there is no evidence to suggest that vitamins taken in excess of normal daily requirements will enhance performance. Nevertheless, there are a number of investigators who recommend that athletes in heavy training should increase their intake of B-vitamins and vitamins C and E (25, 26, 28).

The B-complex vitamins, principally thiamine, play an important role in the metabolism of fats and carbohydrates.

During muscular exercise thiamine requirements may be 15 times greater than at rest. It has been suggested that the daily requirements for vitamin B increase in proportion to the daily energy expenditure (45). Since the caloric intake of training runners generally matches energy expenditure, it is likely that the need for additional B-complex vitamins will be adequately met by the diet, protein foods and whole grains being an excellent source of these vitamins.

The recommendation for vitamin C (ascorbic acid) supplementation also has some theoretical justification. Like the B-complex vitamins, vitamin C has been ascribed a role in oxidative energy metabolism. *In vitro* studies have shown that increased ascorbic acid in blood may result in a shift in the blood oxygen carrying capacity which could make greater amounts of oxygen available to the muscles. Although much of the early literature attributed little advantage to vitamin C supplementation, some recent studies suggest that it may improve physical performance. At this point we can only recognize the controversy and await future findings that can clarify the importance of this vitamin for the distance runner.

It should be noted, however, that vitamin C is necessary to make the "cementing" substance, collagen, which helps hold body cells together. Collagen aids in forming strong scar tissue, important for successful healing of injured muscles and tendons. There is no evidence proving that vitamin C will reduce the likelihood of those injuries common to runners (e.g., muscle and tendon injuries).

Studies by Cureton (26) have proposed that the endurance performance of trained middle-aged men is greater when their diets are supplemented with wheat germ oil, high in vitamin E. However, there has been no demonstration of the beneficial effects of supplemental vitamin E alone. The normal daily food lineup provides about 20-25 units of vitamin E (d-alpha tocopheral), well above that needed by the body (60). The richest sources are vegetable oils, whole grains, and eggs. Nevertheless, the value of vitamin E as an antioxidant is debated with much the same fervor as that of vitamin C and the outcome of the controversy must await further investigation.

In light of this discussion, we can only conclude that vitamin supplementation is of little value to the training athlete, provided he consumes a balanced diet (see reference 45). As pointed out by Astrand and Rodahl (7) ". . . the ingestion of large quantities of vitamin pills is a rather expensive way to increase the vitamin content of the urine. . .”

WATER AND ELECTROLYTE BALANCE

The problem of water and electrolyte losses during exercise has been discussed in Chapter 2. At this point, let us consider the need for replacing the water and salts lost in sweat and urine during repeated days of training.

During periods of intense training, runners may note some day to day variations in body weight, which in most cases is a fluctuation in body water content. By recording the body weight before breakfast each day, excessive water deficits will easily be identified. Since water is sequestered with the glycogen stores, the depletion of muscle and liver glycogen may be reflected in a lower morning weight (0.5-1.0 kg). This weight-water loss can only be replaced with the restoration of glycogen.

There are occasions (e.g., hot weather) when the runner's thirst response is an inadequate gauge of water and electrolyte losses from the extra- and intracellular compartments. As a result, he may become chronically dehydrated. Man's delayed thirst pattern normally causes him to be slow in replacing sweat losses. However, Adolph (2) and others (17) have shown that 24 hours is usually adequate time for men to voluntarily rehydrate. This process may be less complete when runners attempt to train twice each day during warm weather. Under these circumstances, they must force themselves to ingest fluids well in excess of thirst. With such efforts it is possible to replace a 2.8-3.2 kg (6.2-7.0 lbs.) sweat loss in less than 4 hours (22). This means that a runner should be able to rehydrate adequately even when training twice per day.

The problem of replacing the minerals lost in sweat is considerably more complex. Unfortunately, there are no simple methods of judging the body's need for sodium, potassium, chloride, etc. Although some reports have suggested that changes in plasma electrolyte concentrations reflect body excesses and deficits of specific minerals, our recent muscle biopsy studies indicate they do not (16, 71). Probably the most precise method to use in determining body electrolyte balance is that of measuring the intake (diet) and losses (sweat, urine, feces) of various ions over a 24-hour period. The complexity of this procedure makes it nearly impossible to use in a practical

A Scientific Approach to Distance Running

sense, but it can give us some insight into our problem when employed in the laboratory.

In 1974 we studied 10 men and 2 women before, during, and after a 5-day period of heavy training (17). The subjects were required to lose 3% of their body weight (2.2 kg) each day by running and cycling and to eat and drink *ad libitum*. The intake (dietary) and losses (sweat and urine) of water, sodium (Na+), potassium (K+), and chloride (Cl-) were recorded throughout the experiment. Some of these data are presented in Table 3-1. Despite their large sweat losses (2.2 liters/day) electrolyte and water intake more than equaled the total losses (sweat plus urine) incurred during the 5-day period. As a matter of fact, a rather large Na+ and Cl- storage appeared to take place as a result of this sequence. These ions are primarily confined to extracellular compartments (plasma and interstitial fluid). Normally the Na+ content of plasma is maintained quite constant by the kidney. However, during repeated days of

Table 3-1. Water and electrolyte exchange in subjects during five successive days of heavy exercise (10)

Total For 5-Day Training Period

	L O S S E S			Intake Diet	Diff.
	Sweat	Urine	Total		
H_2O (liters)	11.01	4.28	15.29*	17.13**	+1.84
Na^+ (mEq))	391	618	1009	1298	+289
K^+ (mEq)	38	213	251	335	+ 84
Cl^- (mEq)	347	510	857	1005	+148

*Does not include losses by other means (feces, respiration, etc.).
**Does not include H_2O content of food.

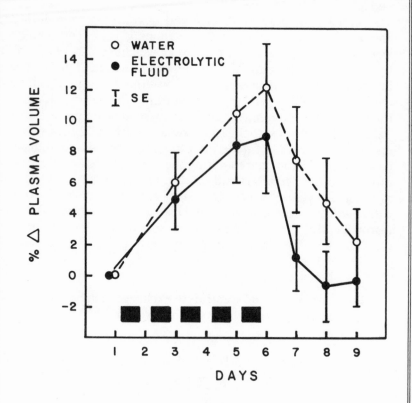

FIGURE 3-3.
EFFECTS OF FIVE DAYS OF HEAVY EXERCISE-SWEATING
ON THE PLASMA VOLUME. MEASUREMENTS WERE
ALSO MADE ON THE FOUR DAYS (6-9) FOLLOWING
THE EXERCISE. BLACK BARS REPRESENT THE
DAYS OF EXERCISE (1-5).

During heavy sweating, extra water is retained in both the plasma and interstitial spaces in order to maintain the plasma Na^+. Thus plasma volume may show a marked increase.

heavy exercise and sweating, the kidney begins to conserve Na+, resulting in an excess of body Na+.

In order to maintain the plasma Na+ concentration within normal limits, extra water is retained in both the plasma and interstitial spaces (17, 82). As a result, plasma volume may show a marked increase (Figure 3-3). Based on the preceding discussion, we have concluded that during repeated days of intense training it is unlikely that runners will incur Na+, or Cl- deficits, provided food intake includes ample electrolytes. However, under circumstances of extremely heavy sweating (losses 6-8% of body weight) runners should consciously increase their daily mineral intake by drinking saline solutions and/or adding extra salt to their food.

It has been charged that intense training programs may induce a sizeable K+ deficit (51, 71). Knochel *et al.* (51) have reported a decrease in total body K+ of 349 mEq in the first 4 days of military training. This would constitute an average daily K+ deficit of 87 mEq per day, despite the fact that the men were ingesting 100 mEq and excreting 46-75 mEq of K+ daily. Since sweat normally contains 4-9 mEq of K+ per liter, then they would be required to lose roughly 20 liters (44 lbs.) of sweat per day to account for the 87 mEq K+ deficit reported by the authors. This is totally impossible and suggests that the K+ deficits reported are the result of some methodological error.

Recently we studied distance runners during two 4-day periods of intense training, 16-32 km (10-20 miles) per day (unpublished). Despite K+ intakes of as little as 25 mEq/day and sweat losses of 3.3 liters/day, the maximum body K+ deficit did not exceed 80 mEq in the 4 days of training. Since the total exchangeable K+ is roughly 3250 mEq, this deficit probably reduced the body K+ by about 2.5%. When the runners ingested a normal K+ (100 mEq/day) diet during training, they remained in positive K+ balance.

We have also examined the losses of calcium and magnesium in sweat, and have found that repeated days of long running do not significantly alter the body content of either ion. As a result of these studies, we have concluded that distance runners do not normally incur electrolyte deficits as a result of successive days of intense training. Compensatory adjustments by the kidney and an ample mineral content of the diet combine to offset the ions lost in sweat and urine.

TRAINING FOR HEAT

Prolonged and repeated training runs in the heat cause a gradual improvement in the runner's ability to tolerate and perform in warm environments. The processes of acclimatization require a number of circulatory and sweat gland adjustments, but can usually be accomplished within 4-8 days (69). It has been noted that heat acclimatization is dependent on the rates of metabolic heat production and the environmental heat stress employed during the acclimatization period (10). Thus, the runner cannot become acclimatized by inactive exposure to the heat but must perform long runs on relatively warm days.

Heat acclimatization is generally characterized by reductions in heart rate and rectal temperature at given environmental temperatures and running speeds (29, 83). Some investigators have even reported decreases in the oxygen requirement during exercise in the heat (83). While these adjustments occur within the first few days of heat-exercise exposure, alterations in sweating are more gradual (52, 68). Improved heat tolerance is associated with an early onset and increased sweat production (53). As a result, skin temperatures are lower, and the gradient between central body and skin temperatures is greater. Thus, less cutaneous (skin) blood flow is required to transfer excess body heat. Although some investigators have found an increase in blood volume in conjunction with heat acclimatization, this is a transitory change and is probably related to the Na+ induced expansion of extracellular water.

What does all this mean to the distance runner, and how can he or she train to gain the greatest benefits? Although the runner must be exposed to the heat to gain full heat acclimatization, he gains partial heat tolerance by training in a cool environment. It should also be noted that when the runner becomes acclimatized for a given heat load, he will be able to perform better at lesser temperatures.

Of greatest importance to the runner is the fact that if he must compete in hot weather, then training should be conducted in the warmest part of the day. Early morning and evening training runs will not fully prepare a distance runner to tolerate the heat of midday. One possible side effect from running in the heat is the requirement it places on muscle glycogen stores. Running at a given speed in the heat will require the utilization of greater amounts of muscle glycogen than the same run in cold air (33). As a result, repeated days of training in the heat may result in an early depletion of glycogen stores and an abnormal chronic state of fatigue.

One final point: heat acclimatization cannot be accelerated by water deprivation. However, maintaining a state of optimal hydration will minimize the hazards of heat injuries and enable the runner to perform more work.

TRAINING FOR ALTITUDE

Since the scheduling of the 1968 Olympic Games in Mexico City, considerable research has been undertaken to describe the acute and chronic effects of moderate altitude (2000-2500 m) on athletic performance (35). Much of the preceding discussion has described man's capacity for endurance exercise under climatic conditions that are relatively compatible with his physiological make-up. However, the atmosphere that houses man is not uniformly optimal for prolonged exhausting running. In light of the vital role played by the oxygen molecule during endurance exercise, it is not surprising that such muscular activity is markedly influenced by the reduced oxygen tension of the air at altitude.

The exchange of oxygen between the alveoli of the lung and the pulmonary blood depends on the difference in the partial pressure of oxygen. When the runner moves from sea level to an elevation of 2500 m (8200 feet), the partial pressure of oxygen in the lung will decrease nearly 30%. Under resting conditions he will probably experience little effect since he will increase his respiratory rate to compensate for the hypoxia of altitude. With the increased demands of distance running, however, pulmonary exchange becomes less adequate, and the limits of oxygen consumption are reduced.

As can be seen in Figure 3-4, maximal oxygen consumption (VO_2 max) decreases roughly 3.2% for each 1000 feet (305 m) increase in altitude above 5000 feet (1524 m). Below 5000 feet it is difficult to detect any decrement in performance or adaptations to prolonged exposure.

Early studies by Pugh (66) demonstrated that the mean time in the three-mile run at Mexico City was 8.5% slower than at sea level. In the mile run, performance decreased 3.6%. This means that a sea level time of 13 minutes for 3 miles would correspond to a 14:07 performance at an altitude of 2300m (7500 ft.).

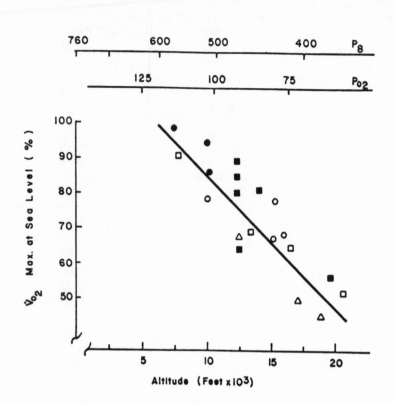

FIGURE 3-4.
THE INFLUENCE OF ALTITUDE (BAROMETRIC
PRESSURE, P_B, AND OXYGEN TENSION P_{O_2})
ON MAXIMAL OXYGEN UPTAKE.

*VO_2 max decreases roughly 3.2% for each 1000 feet (305 m)
increase in altitude above 5000 feet (1524 m). Below 5000 feet,
it is difficult to detect any decrease in performance levels.*

A Scientific Approach to Distance Running

In addition to the lower oxygen tension of the air, altitude offers several other conditions which differ from sea level. The maximal breathing capacity is considerably higher at altitude because of the thinner air (24). The net effect of this reduced resistance to air flow at lowered barometric pressure is a diminished respiratory work to move a given volume of air in and out of the lungs (8).

At the same time there is less air at altitude to resist the movement of the body. This is most noticeable in the sprint events, since air resistance changes with the wind velocity raised to the second power. Another consideration is the relatively cooler, dry air of altitude. Although this will facilitate heat exchange, it also promotes respiratory water loss. As a result, many athletes experience an abrupt body weight loss (i.e., dehydration) during the first few days at altitude, thereby compounding the already reduced capacity for oxygen transport. Finally, solar radiation, which is more intense at altitude, may cause difficulties in the form of sunburn and body temperature regulation during long runs.

The adaptations which result from endurance training at altitude are confined to (1) an increase in pulmonary ventilation, (2) an increase in blood hemoglobin concentration, and (3) functional changes in muscle tissue (e.g., increased oxidative enzymes, myoglobin content and capillarization). During the first few days at altitude the runner will experience a reduced blood alkaline reserve, causing him to be less tolerant of maximal anaerobic effort (72). There is some evidence to show that this may reduce the runner's anaerobic capacity (42).

It is generally agreed that physiological adaptations to altitude are related to the duration of exposure. Since the rate of adaptation is not uniform for all physiological systems, however, full acclimatization to altitude may require several months. Of practical importance is the question, "Can training at altitude improve the distance runner's performance?" Recent studies by Adams, *et al.* (1) have shown that there is no difference in the effects of hard endurance training at 2300m and equivalently severe sea level training on VO_2 max or 2-mile performance time among runners who were already well-conditioned. This is not to say that training at altitude will not improve performance at altitude. To the contrary, after 20 weeks of training at altitude the runners showed marked improvements in their performance at altitude. Sea level performance, however, was unchanged as a result of altitude training.

THE LESSONS LEARNED FROM THE STUDY OF
WORLD-CLASS DISTANCE RUNNERS HAVE APPLICATIONS
TO RUNNERS OF EVERY PERFORMANCE LEVEL.

A Scientific Approach to Distance Running

There appears to be no evidence to support the concept that breathing low oxygen concentrations during brief periods of exercise (1-2 hours per day) will induce even a partial adaptation to altitude (54). It has, however, been demonstrated that this procedure may enhance the maximal exercise breathing capacity.

Since many athletes cannot afford the time or expense involved in long stays at altitude, it is pertinent to consider the study of altitude training by Daniels and Oldridge (27). These researchers concluded that alternate periods of training at 2300m (7-14 days per session) and at sea level (5-11 days each) were adequate stimuli for altitude acclimatization. Sea level stays of up to 11 days did not interfere with the adaptation to altitude as long as training was maintained.

Thus, distance runners who wish to prepare for competition at moderate altitude must realize that (1) full adaptation may require several months, (2) work capacity must be reduced during the initial days at altitude, (3) the rate of acclimatization is unaffected by brief periods at sea level, (4) short exposure to hypobaric conditions is inadequate stimulation for altitude acclimatization, and (5) sea level performance is not improved by altitude (2300m) training in men who are already well trained.

SCIENTIFIC TOOLS FOR THE COACH

We hope that the topics discussed in this book have illustrated the complex individual characteristics of the distance runner and the need to mold a training program to match the specific qualities of each athlete. Obviously, this is easier said than done, since we seldom have all the input necessary to judge the runner's response to training. Nevertheless, let us consider what science could offer the coach who might wish to use the laboratory to develop the runner's full potential.

First, he could consider the muscle fiber composition of the runner's leg muscles. Athletes having less than 60% ST fibers in their gastrocnemius stand little chance of achieving success in national or international distance running competition. Such information could be used to channel hopeful runners into events for which they are genetically best suited. Those with 0 to 40% ST fibers have the greatest potential for sprint running, and those with 40-60% ST are best suited for middle-distance running.

Once identified, the athlete's innate potential for distance running will depend on the physiological adaptations that take place during training. Aside from competitive performance, distance running potential can be judged by measuring the runner's VO_2 max after a month or two of training. It is possible that he may possess a relatively large aerobic capacity but produce only modest performances. One possible cause for such a discrepancy might be that he is an energy-wasting runner. Running economy can be determined by measuring the athlete's oxygen uptake on the treadmill at various speeds and to compare his energy demands to those recorded for other runners at similar speeds. Detailed slow motion film studies of the runner's technique will enable the coach to identify and hopefully correct energy-wasting actions, thereby improving efficiency.

In the course of training, the runner's response to training can be assessed periodically by measuring his VO_2 max. However, repeated measurements should be studied with caution since this test has an error of roughly $\pm$ 3%, a range which could produce a small decrease in VO_2 max that has no physiological significance. After the first 4 to 8 weeks of endurance training, VO_2 max changes very little, yet performance may improve significantly.

Although additional information is needed to substantiate the relationship between distance running performance and changes in muscle enzymes, it seems feasible that in the future coaches could use such enzyme data to evaluate the runner's response to training and to aid in designing a conditioning program to meet the individual needs of the runner.

At the same time the coach might choose to use his knowledge of the runner's % ST muscle fibers to determine the amount of speed and endurance running that should be employed in the runner's training program. Runners having 90-100% ST fibers in their gastrocnemius are likely to lack innate running speed, and will require more speed work (i.e., fast interval running) than distance runners who may have 65% ST fibers.

Such information can also help the coach and runner prepare race tactics. Runners with a high percentage of ST fibers cannot expect to have as fast a finishing sprint as a competitor who has significantly more FT fibers. Thus runners having 90-100% ST fibers must take advantage of these highly oxidative fibers by pushing the pace throughout the

A Scientific Approach to Distance Running

competition. In this way, a competitor with fewer ST fibers will be forced to use his FT fibers in order to maintain contact, thereby diminishing his chances of a strong finishing sprint. Obviously, the reverse pattern should be and often is used by runners having relatively more FT fibers. A slow pace during the race conserves the potential speed of his FT fibers, which can then be called upon for the finishing sprint.

To insure that runners have an adequate storage of muscle glycogen, the coach can again use both biochemical and nutritional data to form a proper training program and diet for each runner. Since heavy training and inadequate carbohydrate intake can lead to poor performances, measurements of muscle glycogen can identify and assist in the treatment of chronic exhaustion associated with low muscle glycogen.

Of course, other physiological, anatomical, and environmental measurements can be made by the coach and runner to help in designing a sound training program and at the same time enable the runner to more closely approach his ultimate potential. Some of the factors to be considered include the following:

(1) Body fat content. This should not exceed 8% for males and 15% for females.

(2) Dehydration. Body weight should be recorded each morning before breakfast. Sudden weight loss (more than 1.0 kg) may reflect inadequate fluid replacement, low muscle glycogen storage and physical staleness.

(3) Excessive environmental heat stress. Air temperature, relative humidity, and radiant heat (sun) should be considered when planning the training session during warm weather. Rectal temperatures in excess of 40° C (104° F) after training or competition suggest that the runner has difficulty dissipating body heat under the conditions (running speed and environmental heat stress) of that run. Thus, given similar environmental conditions the coach must anticipate the runner's limitations and reduce speed and/or running distance.

SUMMARY

Despite the current body of knowledge acquired through research, coaching the distance runner still remains an art. The individual variations in the runner's psychology, physiology, and anatomy make it impossible to design a single training program that will meet the needs of all distance runners. Nevertheless, many important questions have been answered.

The objective of every distance running coach should be to develop the ultimate natural potential of each runner. This is compatible with the goals of the sports scientist. Unlike the trial and error methods of traditional coaching, present and future scientific findings will provide the coach and runner with information essential for the runner to take the best advantage of his innate and cultivated capacities for distance running.

REFERENCES

1. Adams, W.C., Bernauer, E.M., Dill, D.B. and Bomar, J.B. Effects of equivalent sea-level and altitude training on VO_2 max and running performance. *J. Appl. Physiol.* 39: 262-266, 1975.
2. Adolph, E.F. *Physiology of Man in the Desert.* New York: Interscience, 1947.
3. Asprey, G.M., Alley, L.E., and Tuttle, W.W. Effect of eating at various times upon subsequent performances in the one-mile run. *Res. Quart.* 35:227-230, 1964.
4. Asprey, G.M., Alley, L.E., and Tuttle, W.W. Effect of eating at various times upon subsequent performances in the two-mile run. *Res. Quart.* 36:233-236, 1965.
5. Astrand, P.-O. *Experimental studies of physical working capacity in relation to age and sex.* Copenhagen, Ejnar Munksgaard, 1952.
6. Astrand, P.-O., Cuddy, T., Saltin, B. and Stenberg, J. Cardiac output during submaximal and maximal work. *J. Appl. Physiol.* 19:268-274, 1964.
7. Astrand, P.-O. and Rodahl, K. *Textbook of Work Physiology.* New York, McGraw-Hill, p. 483, 1970.
8. Astrand, P.-O. and Rodahl, K. *Textbook of Work Physiology.* New York, McGraw-Hill, p. 563, 1970.
9. Bartels, R. Interval training and cardiorespiratory conditioning. Abstract AAHPER National Convention, 1968.
10. Bass, D.E. Thermoregulatory and circulatory adjustments during acclimatization to heat in man. In: *Temperature: Its Measurement and Control in Science and Industry.* (Edited by J.D. Hardy). New York: Rheinhold Publishing Corp., 1963. Vol. 3, Part 3.
11. Bergstrom, J., and Hultman, E. Muscle glycogen synthesis after exercise: An enhancing factor localized to the muscle cells in man. *Nature.* 210:309-310, 1966.
12. Bevegard, B.S. and Shepherd, J.T. Regulation of the circulation during exercise in man. *Physiol. Rev.* 47:178, 1967.
13. Buick, F.J., Gledhill, N., Froese, A.B., and Spriet, E.C. Double blind study of blood boasting in highly trained runners. (Abstract) *Med. Sci. Sports.* 10:49, 1978.
14. Buskirk, E.R. and Moore, R. Exercise and body fluids. In: *Science and Medicine of Exercise and Sport* (ed. W.R. Johnson). New York: Harper and Brothers, 1960.
15. Costill, D.L., Bowers, R., Branam, G. and Sparks, K. Muscle glycogen utilization during prolonged exercise on successive days. *J. Appl. Physiol.* 31:834-838, 1971.
16. Costill, D.L., Cote, R., Fink, W. and Van Handel, P.J. Water and electrolyte changes in active and inactive muscle during prolonged exercise. *J. Appl. Physiol.* (In Press).

A Scientific Approach to Distance Running

17. Costill, D.L., Cote, R., Miller, E., Miller, T. and Wynder, S. Water and electrolyte replacement during repeated days of work in the heat. *Aviat. Space Environ. Med.* 46:795-800, 1975.

18. Costill, D.L., Daniels, J., Evans, W., Fink, W., Krahenbuhl, G. and Saltin, B. Skeletal muscle enzymes and fiber composition in male and female track athletes. *J. Appl. Physiol.* (In Press).

19. Costill, D.L., Fink, W. and Pollock, M. Muscle fiber composition and enzyme activities of elite distance runners. *Med. Sci. Sports.* 8:96-100, 1976.

20. Costill, D.L., and Fox, E.L. Energetics of marathon running. *Med. Sci. Sports.* 1:81-86, 1969.

21. Costill, D.L., Gollnick, P.D., Jansson, E.D., Saltin, B. and Stein, E.M. Glycogen depletion pattern in human muscle fibers during distance running. *Acta physiol. scand.* 89:374-383, 1973.

22. Costill, D.L. and Sparks, K.E. Rapid fluid replacement following dehydration. *J. Appl. Physiol.* 34:299-303, 1973.

23. Costill, D.L., Winrow, E. Maximal oxygen intake among marathon runners. *Arch. Phys. Med. Rehab.* 51:317-320, 1970.

24. Cotes, J.E. Ventilatory capacity at altitude and its relation to mask design. *Proc. Roy. Soc.* (London), ser. B. 143-32-37, 1954.

25. Crandon, J.H., Lund, C.C., and Dill, D.B. Experimental human scurvy. *New Eng. J. Med.* 223-353-357, 1940.

26. Cureton, T.K. Effect of wheat germ oil and vitamin E on normal human subjects in physical training programs. *Am. J. Physiol.* 179-628-632, 1954.

27. Daniels, J. and Oldridge, N. The effects of alternate exposure to altitude and sea level on World-Class middle-distance runners. *Med. Sci. Sports.* 2:107-112, 1970.

28. Egana, E., Johnson, R.E., Bloomfield, R., Brouha, L., Meiklejohn, A.P., Whittenberger, J., Darling, R.C., Heath, C., Graybeil, A. and Consolazio, J. The effects of a diet deficiency in the vitamin B complex on sedentary men. *Am. J. Physiol.* 127-731-740, 1942.

29. Eichma, L.W., and others. Thermal regulation during acclimatization to hot, dry environment. *Amer. J. Physiol.* 163-585, 1950.

30. Ekblom, B., Astrand, P. -O., Saltin, B., Stenberg, J. and Wallstrom, B. Effect of training on circulatory response to exercise. *J. Appl. Physiol.* 24:518-582, 1968.

31. Ekblom, B., Goldbarg, A.N. and Gullbring, B. Response to exercise after blood loss and reinfusion. *J. Appl. Physiol.* 33:175-180, 1972.

32. Eriksson, B.O., Gollnick, P.D. and Saltin, B. Muscle metabolism and enzyme activities after training in boys 11-13 years old. *Acta physiol. scand.* 87:231-239, 1972.

33. Fink, W., Costill, D.L., and Van Handel, P. Leg muscle metabolism during exercise in the heat and cold. *Europ. J. Appl. Physiol.* 34:183-190, 1975.

34. Fox, E.L., Bartels, R.L., Billings, C.E., Mathews, D.K., Bason, R. and Webb, W.M. Intensity and distance of interval training programs and changes in aerobic power. *Med. Sci. Sports.* 5:18-22, 1973.

35. Goddard, R.F. *The Effects of Altitude on Physical Performance,* Chicago: The Athletic Institute, 1967.

36. Gollnick, P.D., Armstrong, R.B., Saltin, B., Saubert, C.W., Sembrowich, W.L. and Shephard, R.E. Effect of training on enzyme activities and fiber composition of human skeletal muscle. *J. Appl. Physiol.* 34:107-111, 1973.

37. Gollnick, P.D., Armstrong, R.B., Saubert IV, C.W., Sembrowich, W.L., Shephard, R.E. and Saltin, B. Glycogen depletion patterns in human skeletal muscle fibers during prolonged work. *Pfluger Arch.* 344-1-12, 1973.

38. Gollnick, P.D., Ianuzzo, D.C. and King, D.W. Ultrastructural and enzyme changes in muscles with exercise. In: *Muscle Metabolism During Exercise.* (Ed. Pernow, B. and Saltin, B.) New York: Plenum Press, pp. 69-85, 1971.

39. Gollnick, P.D. and King, D.W. Energy release in the muscle cell. *Med. Sci. Sports.* 1:23-31, 1969.

40. Grimby, G., Haggendahl, E. and Saltin, B. Local Xenom 133 clearance from the quadriceps muscle during exercise in man. *J. Appl. Physiol.* 22:305-310, 1967.
41. Grimby, G. and Saltin, B. A physiological analysis of still active middle-aged and old athletes. *Acta Med. Scand.* 179:513-520, 1966.
42. Hansen, J.E., Stelter, G.P. and Vogel, J.A. Arterial pyruvate, lactate, pH, and P_{CO_2} during work at sea level and high altitude. *J. Appl. Physiol.* 23-523-526, 1967.
43. Holloszy, J.O., Oscai, L.B., Don, I.J., and Mole, P.A. Mitochondrial citric acid cycle and related enzymes: Adaptive responses to exercise. *Biochem. Biophys. Res. Comm.* 40:1368-1373, 1970.
44. Holloszy, J.O., Oscai, L.B., Mole, P.A. and Don, I.J. Biochemical adaptations to endurance exercise in skeletal muscle. In: *Muscle Metabolism During Exercise.* (Ed. Pernow, B. and Saltin, B.), New York: Plenum Press, pp. 51-61, 1971.
45. Horstman. D.H. Nutrition. In: *Ergogenic Aids and Muscular Performance.* (Ed. Morgan, W.P.), New York: Academic Press.
46. Hultman, E., and Bergstrom, J. Muscle glycogen synthesis in relation to diet studied in normal subjects. *Acta Med. Scand.* Supplement, 1967.
47. Hultman, E. and Nilsson, L.H. Liver glycogen in man. Effects of different diets and muscular exercise. In: *Muscle Metabolism During Exercise.* (Ed. Pernow, B. and Saltin, B.), New York: Plenum Press, pp. 69-85, 1971.
48. Kiessling, K.H., Piehl, K. and Lundquist, C.G. Effect of physical training on ultrastructural features in human skeletal muscle. In: *Muscle Metabolism During Exercise.* (Ed. Pernow, B. and Saltin, B.), New York: Plenum Press, pp. 97-101, 1971.
49. Kjellberg, S.R., Rudhe, U. and Sjostrand, T. Increase of the amount of hemoglobin and blood volume in connection with physical training. *Acta physiol. scand.* 19:146-154, 1949.
50. Kjellberg, S.R., Ruhde, U. and Sjostrand, T. The amount of hemoglobin and the blood volume in relation to the pulse rate and cardiac volume during rest. *Acta physiol. scand.* 19:136-145, 1949.
51. Knochel, J.P., Dotin, L.N. and Hamburger, R. Pathophysiology of intense physical conditioning in a hot climate. *J. Clin. Invest.* 51:242-255, 1972.
52. Kuno, Y. *Human Perspiration.* Springfield, Illinois. Charles C. Thomas, 1956.
53. Leithead, C.S. and Lind, A.R. *Heat Stress and Heat Disorders.* London: Cassell and Company, 1964.
54. Loeppky. J.A. and Bynum, W.A. Effects of periodic exposure to hypobaria and exercise on physical work capacity. *J. Sports Med. and Phys. Fitness.* 10:238-247.
55. Lumian, N.C., and Krumdick, V.F. Physiological, psychological aspects of marathon training for distance runners. *Athletic J.* 45:68, 1965.
56. Mirwald, R.L. A comparison of the effectiveness of training middle-distance runners by the Swedish system and the Oregon system. Unpublished Master's Thesis. Eugene: University of Oregon, 1965.
57. Morgan, T.E., Short, F.A. and Cobb, L.A. Effect of long-term exercise on human muscle mitochondria. In: *Muscle Metabolism During Exercise.* (Ed. Pernow, B. and Saltin, B.) New York: Plenum Press, pp. 97-101, 1971.
58. Morgan, T.E., Short, F.A. and Cobb, L.A. Effect of long-term exercise on skeletal muscle lipid composition. *Amer. J. Physiol.* 216-82-86, 1969.
59. Noon, T.J. The effects of speed training and overdistance training on young runners. Unpublished Master's Thesis. San Diego: San Diego State College, 1963.
60. *Nutrition For Athletes.* American Association for Health, Physical Education and Recreation. Washington, D.C., pp. 53-55, 1971.
61. Oscai, L.B. and Holloszy, J.O. Biochemical adaptations in muscle: II. Response of mitochondrial adenosine triphosphatase, creatine phospokinase, and adenylate kinase activities in skeletal muscle to exercise. *J. Biol. Chem.*

246-6968-6972, 1971.

62. Petren, T., Sjostrand, T. and Syleven, G. Der Einfluss des Training auf die Haufigkeit der Kapillaren in Herz und Skeletmuskulatar. *Arbeitsphysiol.* 9:376-385, 1936.

63. Piehl, K. Time course for glycogen storage in muscle fibers of man following exercise-induced depletion. *Acta physiol. scand.* (In Press).

64. Pollock, M.L., Broida, J., Kendrick, Z., Miller, Jr., H.S., Janeway, R. and Linnerud, A.C. Effects of training two days per week at different intensities on middle-aged men. *Med. Sci. Sports.* 4:192-197, 1972.

65. Pollock, M.L., Cureton, T.K., and Greninger, L. Effects of frequency of training on working capacity, cardiovascular function, and body composition of adult men. *Med. Sci. Sports.* 1:70-74, 1969.

66. Pugh, L.G.C.E. Athletes at altitude. *J. Physiol.* 192:619-747, 1967.

67. Robertson, R., Gilcher, R., Metz, K., Bahnson, H., Allison, T., Skrinar, G., Abbott, A., and Becker, R. Effect of red cell reinfusion on physical working capacity and perceived exertion at normal and reduced oxygen pressure. (Abstract). *Med. Sci. Sports.* 10:49, 1978.

68. Robinson, S. Circulatory adjustment of men in hot environments. In: *Temperature: It's Measurement and Control in Science and Industry.* (Edited by J.D. Hardy). New York: Rheinhold Publishing Corp., 1963. Vol. 3, Part 3.

69. Robinson, S. Training, acclimatization and heat tolerance. In: *Proceedings of the International Symposium on Physical Activity and Cardiovascular Health.* Toronto, Ontario, Canada. October 11-13, 1966.

70. Rogan, T. A comparative investigation of the values of supplementing a daily training program with a second training session of continuous running. Master's Thesis. Muncie, Indiana: Ball State University, 1968.

71. Rose, K.D. Warning for millions: Intense exercise can deplete potassium. *Physician Sports Med.* 3(5):26-29, 1975.

72. Roughton, F. J.W. Transport of oxygen and carbon dioxide. In: *Handbook of Physiology* (Ed. Fenn, W.O. and Rahn, H.) Sec. 3, Respiration, Vol. 1, p. 767, American Physiological Society, Washington, D.C., 1964.

73. Rowell, L.B. Factors affecting the prediction of the maximal oxygen intake from measurements made during submaximal work. Doctoral dissertation. University of Minnesota, 1962.

74. Saltin, B. *Intermittent Exercise: Its Physiology and Practical Application.* (Lecture) Published by Ball State University, Muncie, Indiana, 1975, in booklet form.

75. Saltin, B. Physiological effects of physical conditioning. *Med. Sci. Sports.* 1:50-56, 1969.

76. Saltin, B., Blomqvist, G., Mitchell, J.H., Johnson, R.L., Wildenthal, K., and Chapman, C.B. Response to exercise after bedrest and after training. *Circulation* Suppl. 7, 1968.

77. Saltin, B., Costill, D.L., Stein, E., Narzanar, K., Jansson, E., Essen, B., and Gollnick, P.D. The nature of a training response: peripheral and general adaptations to one-legged exercise. *Acta physiol. scand.* (In Press).

78. Saubert. C.W., Armstrong, R.B., Shephard, R.E. and Gollnick, P.D. Anaerobic enzyme adaptations to sprint training in rats. *Pflugers Arch.* 341-305-312, 1973.

79. Shrubb, A.A. Long distance running. *Training for Athletics.* London: Health and Strength, Ltd., 1904, pp. 46-53.

80. Sjostrand, T. Functional capacity and exercise tolerance in patients with impaired cardiovascular function. In: *Clinical Cardiopulmonary Physiology.* New York: Grane and Shattar, Inc., 1960.

81. Sjostrand, T. The total quantity of hemoglobin in man and its relation to age, sex, body weight, height. *Acta physiol. scand.* 18:325-333, 1949.

82. Smiles, K.A., and Robinson, S. Sodium ion conservation during acclimatization of men to work in the heat. *J. Appl. Physiol.* 31:63-69, 1971.

83. Strydom, N.B., and others. Acclimatization to humid heat and the role of physical conditioning. *J. Appl. Physiol.* 21:636-642, 1966.

84. Taylor, H.L., Buskirk, E., and Henschel, A. Maximal oxygen intake as an objective measure of cardiorespiratory performance. *J. Appl. Physiol.* 8:73-81, 1955.

85. Van Huss, W., and others. Effects of mild consumption on endurance performance. *Res. Quart.* 33:120-128, 1962.

86. Williams, M.H., Goodwin, A.R., Perkins, R. and Bocrie, J. Effect of blood reinjection upon endurance capacity and heart rate. *Med. Sci. Sports.* 5:181-186, 1973.

87. Zeigler, R.G. The frequency of maximum effort most favorable to the development of endurance in college students. Master's Thesis. University Park: Pennsylvania State University, 1960.

TRAINING AND PREPARATION FOR COMPETITION

Now let us apply our scientific knowledge in an effort to gain the utmost from the runner's inherent and often untapped talents. From the preceding discussion it should now be quite apparent that there are many gaps in our understanding of the physiological adaptations which occur during endurance training. Our lack of understanding and the wide individual variations in response to training make it difficult to predict the outcome of any training regimen. Thus, efforts to describe an "ideal" training program for the distance runner must be set forth with many qualifications and numerous alternatives. Nevertheless, there are a number of scientifically based principles that are applicable to most distance training programs.

In the past, coaches and runners have mimicked the training regimens of current champions. While there is obvious logic in this approach, it represents a risky "trial and error method" for the runner who lacks the physical and psychological profile of the champion. That is not to say that many sound principles cannot be gained from the elite runner. To the contrary, many of the training guidelines used by successful distance runners can be applied to the eager novice, provided they are scaled down to meet his lesser abilities, experience, and recuperative powers.

A personal experience might help to emphasize this point. My career as a distance running coach was confined to a group of talented, but certainly undeveloped, college cross-country runners. One of the most talented runners in this group was a young man extremely eager to compete at a national level. As a result, he followed the training programs described for some of the best world-class runners. There was little surprise that his performances improved rapidly, resulting in several national championships within the first four years of his competition. His efforts, however, were fraught with problems: pulled achilles tendons, knee injuries, and often erratic performances. In retrospect, it seems that the stress of such training was far in excess of his physical and psychological tolerance. Too often such injuries are accepted as the "price one must pay" for success. Fortunately, however, our knowledge of the growth changes associated with endurance training tells us that such costs are unnecessary. With proper planning, progression, and preventive measures, the same goals can be achieved with a minimum of pathological trauma and fewer erratic performances.

IDENTIFYING THE RUNNER'S POTENTIAL

Unlike sprint running, the beginning distance runner's endurance potential can only be assessed after months of training. Only in this way can we test his/her inherent capacity to adapt to training. Naturally, a muscle biopsy taken from the gastrocnemius (calf) and/or the vastus lateralis (thigh) muscles could identify those athletes who are less likely prospects for the longest races. A histo-chemical stain (myosin ATP-ase) to determine the muscle's fiber composition (slow and fast twitch) can aid in channeling runners into the events for which they are best suited. Those whose muscles contain less than 40% slow twitch (ST) fibers should be encouraged to concentrate on events shorter than 800m, while those with 40-60% ST fibers should direct their attention to the 800 and 1500m events. The group of individuals having the greatest potential for success in distance running are those having more than 60% ST fibers.

After a period of initial training, we can again turn to the laboratory for additional input that will tell us more about the athlete's endurance potential. Two specific items of information are useful in this respect. The first is a measure of the runner's maximal oxygen uptake (VO_2 max) capacity. Although not fully developed after such a brief period of training, it can provide some insight concerning the runner's endurance potential. Although most "top flight" male distance runners have VO_2 max values in excess of 70 ml/kg-min^{-1}, we find that with only 1-2 months of training the better prospects have VO_2 values in excess of 65 ml/kg-min^{-1}. Potential female distance runners, on the other hand, are generally 5-8 ml/kg-min^{-1} less than their male counterparts at this point of conditioning.

What about the age of the runner? So long as the prospect is older than 15 years, the preceding rating scale seems to be a good predictor of future success. As a matter of fact, we have even measured VO_2 max values in excess of 70 ml/kg-min^{-1} among 13 and 14 year-old boys. Despite additional growth and significant improvements in running performances, these subjects showed little change in VO_2 max.

Since we have already pointed out the important role played by oxygen in successful endurance performance (Chapter 1) you might wonder, "How can runners improve their performance without increasing their capacity to consume oxygen?" One obvious way is to become more efficient, thus requiring less oxygen to run at any given speed. As a result, a third laboratory test involves the measurement of oxygen consumption at various running speeds. In our laboratory, the runners perform a series of seven-minute runs at 200, 240, 268 and/or 322 m/min (7.5, 9.0, 10.0 and 12.0 mph), depending on the runner's ability. During the run both oxygen consumption and heart rates are monitored, and the averaged data from 5 to 7 minutes of exercise are selected to represent the values for each running speed.

Figure 4-1 offers an opportunity to judge the relative efficiency of the runner. Although it is an obvious advantage to be very efficient, one should not lose sight of the fact that running efficiency will change with training and improved technical skills. The importance of running efficiency cannot be emphasized too strongly. While VO_2 max seems to reach its full potential within a few months after the start of training, reducing the cost of submaximal running may take years to develop fully.

Since in the performance of distance running both VO_2 max and efficiency are critical components for success, it is best to compare the runner's laboratory data in relative terms. That

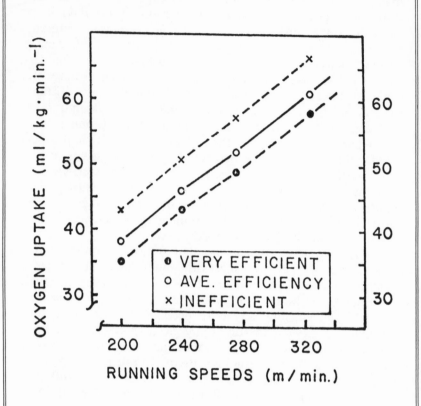

FIGURE 4-1.
CHANGES IN RUNNING EFFICIENCY AS MEASURED
BY OXYGEN UPTAKE (ML/KG X MIN.)
AT VARIOUS RUNNING SPEEDS (M/MIN.).

Running efficiency is one factor which can be improved over time, and which will in turn improve performance levels.

110

is, we must examine the percentage of VO_2 max at a given speed to determine the ahtlete's immediate and future potential. For example, let us study the laboratory data for the two runners listed below.

	Runner 1	Runner 2
VO_2 max (ml/kg X min.)	70.0	65.0
VO_2 at 268 m/min.	55.0	48.0
% VO_2 max at 268 m/min.	79%	74%

Although runner #2 has a lower VO_2 max than runner #1, his relative effort in running at 268 m/min is such that he uses less of his oxygen uptake capacity to run at that speed (6 min/mile). As a result, the sensation of effort is less and his potential for maintaining that pace for prolonged periods is greater than runner #1.

STUDIES OF DISTANCE RUNNERS INDICATE THERE IS NO SINGLE PREDICTOR OF SUCCESS— "TALENT" IS A COMPOSITE OF MANY FACTORS.

At this point we have eliminated some athletes who lack the obvious prerequisites for success in distance running. From a philosophical point of view, these methods of selection are not designed to exclude those from participating who find distance running a source of enjoyment despite their limited proficiency. It does, however, suggest that those who seek to be winners in endurance activities, although they lack the prerequisites, may find greater success in other forms of sport.

Once the runner's potential talents have been weighed, it is time to gather information that will be useful in designing a training program that takes into account an individual's ability to tolerate repeated days of heavy training. The only method known to judge the runner's recuperative powers is experience. Although measurements of muscle glycogen and blood hemoglobin concentrations may sound the alarm of overtraining, the runner's sensations of effort and the stopwatch are more reliable indices of staleness. The best way to determine a runner's required ratio of training to rest is to keep a training diary of mileage/intensity, performance, and subjective observations. This point, however, may take a bit of study since the answer may read like a puzzle. There are a variety of factors which complicate our efforts to determine how many days a runner can train hard before needing a day or two of light training or complete rest. Aside from the acute effects of diet, training intensity and enviornmental heat stress, general muscular fatigue may be acquired in an accumulative manner over a period of weeks. Too often we examine only the immediate demands of an isolated training bout in search of the causes of overtraining.

In general, most runners can tolerate two hard days of training followed by a lighter training day or complete rest. Some individuals may find it best to run hard on alternate days, while others can handle three or four heavy days of training. Naturally, years of running experience and advanced levels of fitness enhance one's tolerance to repeated days of hard training. Herein lies the secret to the full value of any training program.

Too often both coach and runner ignore the important contribution of rest to running performance. From a physiological point of view, the purpose of physical training is to stimulate the biological systems essential for prolonged, high rates of energy production. As a result, the systems are often overused and require rest to compensate for the stresses of

A Scientific Approach to Distance Running

training. It is in this way that the systems get stronger and the runner's endurance improves. Thus, rest is an equally important part of the training program, for without it the system will certainly fail.

GENERAL TRAINING GUIDELINES

Aside from the need for adequate rest, there are a number of other guidelines which provide a strong basis for the training program. First, the coach and/or runner should establish a long-term general plan for the program. This should be a one or two-year projection of the runner's development. Of course, in the first year of a runner's career when improvements are rapid it is difficult to anticipate the rate of adaptation to training. For that reason, any plans outlined for the runner should be flexible and frequently adjusted. The longitudinal approach to training should be based on a logical *progression,* with a gradual increase in training stress.

Based on previous research, it seems that the total work performed serves as the strongest stimulus for an endurance training response. This fact supports the current emphasis placed on the total running distance performed in a given week. This training philosophy, however, forces the runner to attempt similar weekly efforts, with little opportunity to insert extremely long runs or to lighten the training effort when needed. Since most physiological systems require three to four weeks to show a response to a given training stress, it seems the runner's training load should be judged on the basis of total distance covered in a four-week period. This system offers the advantage of varying the weekly running effort, while permitting longer periods of light training to allow full recovery from overdistance and/or intense efforts. The latter point is important, since it often requires more than a few days to recover from an extremely taxing period of difficult training.

Consequently, the weekly training sequence for a runner might follow the pattern shown in Figure 4-2. As illustrated, each cycle required the greatest distance during the second and fourth weeks with marked reduction in total effort during the first and third weeks. In this way, the runner gains the full benefit of the most difficult training periods by permitting more complete recovery. In the most experienced runners the contrast between the weekly distances need not be so great. However, in every four-week cycle the runner would have one

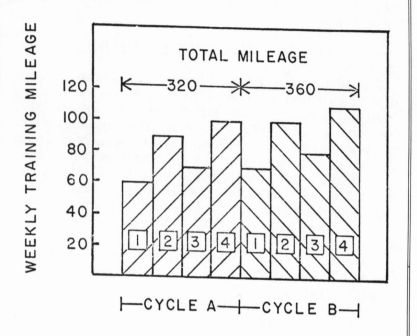

FIGURE 4-2.
TRAINING SEQUENCE FOR A RUNNER DEMONSTRATING
ALTERATIONS IN WEEKLY MILEAGE TO ALLOW
FOR BOTH PROGRESSION AND RECOVERY.

Each cycle requires the greatest distance during the second and fourth weeks, with marked reduction in total effort during the first and third weeks. Thus, the runner gains the full benefit of the difficult training sessions by permitting a more complete recovery.

A Scientific Approach to Distance Running

week of relatively light training (e.g., 50-60% of the distance covered on week 4 of the previous cycle). It should be pointed out that this method of varying the weekly training effort was first described by Bill Bowerman (University of Oregon) and is currently quite popular in a number of European countries. When compared to other training plans this system offers several major advantages and definite scientific support.

Within each week of training the runner should utilize both long, *endurance type runs* and *intermittent bouts* of running at speeds equal to or faster than racing pace. In the non-competitive periods of training the number of days and/or workouts used for intermittent speed work can be limited to one per week. During competitive periods of training, the number of such sessions should be increased to two or three per week. The pace used during these intermittent bouts will be discussed in some detail later (Specific Details of Training).

For the distance runner, repeated bouts of speed work serves two important functions. First it increases the tension requirements for the running muscles, thereby simulating the recruitment of muscle fibers that will be used during competition. Without training runs at race pace or faster some muscle fibers needed during the race will receive little training. Remember, training runs at slower than racing pace will place the greatest emphasis on the slow twitch (ST) fibers. Higher intensity running will demand the use of both the ST and fast twitch (FT) fibers.

The second major contribution of intermittent training is that it promotes efficient running at the pace demands of competition. The subtle interaction and patterns of leg muscle contractions, arm and leg rotations, muscle relaxation, stride length, and vertical displacement of the center of gravity are important in the economical use of energy during running. Training at speeds which approximate racing pace will aid the runner in coordinating his/her efforts to perform efficiently.

SPECIFIC DETAILS OF TRAINING

Certainly the fine *art* of coaching a distance runner depends on the ability to match the training program to meet the experience and physical talents of the runner. In an effort to apply the specific details of training to the variety of individual abilities, the following discussion will cover training for beginning, intermediate and elite runners.

The program for the beginning runner assumes that he/she is within the first year of organized training and has experienced little or no competition. Neither the age nor sex of the runner is of concern in planning a training program for this group, since there is no evidence to suggest that there is any difference in the adaptations of men, women, young or middle-age to endurance training. Obviously, the runner's initial tolerance of heavy training will depend on physical fitness and innate potential. At the same time, however, not all runners will adjust to the training stress at the same rate or to the same degree.

"Overtraining" probably constitutes the greatest single error made in the management of the beginning runner. In light of the high rate of injury, emotional staleness and physical exhaustion which often accompany overtraining, the first principle to remember is to begin training at a very low level, estimated to be well within the runner's capacity. If after the first training sessions the runner develops muscle soreness, the work is too difficult. Should the runner find it impossible to complete the training distance or to maintain the training pace, the total training effort should be reduced. Symptoms of overtraining generally include restless sleep, loss of appetite, reduced performance, and elevated resting heart rate. These responses are applicable to runners with varied levels of experience, and generally demand several days to a week of reduced work or complete rest.

Discussion of specific aspects of the training program must be qualified in terms of both immediate and long-range objectives. The basic strength of any program is established in the non-competitive phase of training. It is during this period of training that the runner can subject him/her self to heavy exercise stress without the fear of affecting performance. The non-competitive phase of training is considered to be the period of major physiological development. This does not necessarily mean that good running performances will be experienced in conjunction with such heavy training stress. To the contrary, performances will be substantially less than the runner's actual potential. Thus there exists a need for a second style of training that will permit the runner to maintain a high level of fitness and optimize his/her performance. Training during the competitive season, therefore, should allow for full recovery from heavy training with specific emphasis placed on running at racing speeds or faster.

116

In general, the two types of training (non-competitive and competitive) differ in both the quality and quantity of work performed. Non-competitive training should emphasize distance at speeds considerably slower than racing pace. In physiological terms this means at running speeds that will require the consumption of oxygen at roughly 60-70% of the runner's oxygen uptake capacity (% VO_2 max) (See Table 4-1).

During the competitive phase of training the total weekly running distance is markedly reduced, while the quality of the effort is increased. Distance runs during this period should place greater demands on the oxygen transport system, requiring 75-85% VO_2 max. As can be seen in Table 4-2, both the number of sessions and the running speeds performed during the intermittent type workouts are increased during the competitive phase of training. In this way the demands of training more closely simulate the energy requirements and movement patterns required for competitive performance.

Training programs for the novice and elite runners differ only in the rate and distance of running. As you may recall from our previous discussion (Chapter 2), the price paid for speed is a reduction in the total distance that can be covered in training and an increase in the quantity of muscle glycogen used. Since the term "speed" is relative to the runner's ability to consume oxygen maximally, it is more accurate to describe the desired training pace in terms of the percentage of the runner's maximal oxygen uptake (% VO_2 max). Obviously not everyone has a laboratory available to help judge the runner's % VO_2 max at various running speeds. For that reason it might be helpful to give some practical indicators (Table 4-1).

Thus, the runner's pace during distance races can be used to approximate his/her % VO_2 max. As an example, let us assume that during training we want to perform repeated 800m runs at 80% of VO_2 max, the same pace required during a 10-mile race. If we assume that the runner has a best 10-mile time of 60 min (6 min/mile), then the 800m repeat runs would be performed at roughly 3 minutes each.

Table 4-2 provides an example of the type of training that will establish a strong endurance base (non-competitive training) and the necessary sharpening for optimal race performance (competitive training). It should be noted, however, that this training format is offered only to illustrate the relative emphasis on distance and speed running. Obviously, beginning runners

TABLE 4-1.   ESTIMATES OF THE PERCENTAGE OF ONE'S MAXIMAL OXYGEN UPTAKE (% VO_2 MAX) USED AT DIFFERENT RUNNING SPEEDS.

Speed* Required to Perform at Various Distances	Estimated % VO_2 Required
Average Pace for 1 mile or 1500 m	115 - 130%
Average Pace for 2 mile or 3000 m	95 - 100%
Average Pace for 4 mile or 5000 m	90 - 95%
Average Pace for 6 mile or 10km	85 - 90%
Average Pace for 10 mile or 15km	80 - 85%
Average Pace for the Marathon	75 - 80%

*Denotes Best Performance

may only be able to cover 30-40 miles per week, while the elite, experienced runner may be capable of managing more than 100 miles per week. Two aspects of both runners' programs can, however, remain similar. Generally, all runners can train at the same % VO_2 max and probably should include a similar number of intermittent work sessions per week. That is not to say that they should all run at the same speed. Naturally, if two runners run at the same % VO_2 max, the runner with the highest oxygen uptake capacity will have to run faster than the second runner. Thus, the speed requirements during training are a function of the runner's physiological capacity, which improves gradually with conditioning. For that reason the training load should show a gradual progression (see Figure 4-2), keeping pace with the runner's capacity, but not exceeding it.

TABLE 4-2. EXAMPLES OF TRAINING SCHEDULES DURING THE NON-COMPETITIVE (NC) AND COMPETITIVE (C) PHASES OF A RUNNER'S CONDITIONING PROGRAM. ALL DISTANCE RUNNING DURING THE NC PERIODS IS PERFORMED AT 60-70% OF THE RUNNER'S OXYGEN UPTAKE CAPACITY (% VO$_2$ MAX). INTERMITTENT WORK BOUTS SHOULD BE RUN AT 85-90% VO$_2$ MAX, WITH REST INTERVALS EQUAL TO THE EXERCISE PERIODS.

NON-COMPETITIVE PHASE

Day of Week	WEEK 1	WEEK 2	WEEK 3	WEEK 4
1	10 miles	15 miles	15 miles	20 miles
2	5 "	5 "	5 "	5 "
3 a.m.	4 "	8 "	6 "	8 "
p.m.	4 x 800 m	4 x 1 mile	4 x 800 m	6 x 1 mile
4	10 miles	12 miles	10 miles	12 miles
5	8 "	10 "	8 "	10 "
6	10 "	12 "	10 "	15 "
7	6 "	10 "	6 "	8 "

Total Weekly Mileage

	55 miles	76 miles	62 miles	84 miles

COMPETITIVE PHASE

Day of Week	WEEK 1	WEEK 2	WEEK 3	WEEK 4
1	10 miles	10 miles	10 miles	10 miles
2 a.m.	8 miles	6 x 1 mile x 100%	8 miles	7 x 1 mile x 100%
p.m.	15 x 400m x 125%	8 miles	15 x 400m x 125%	8 miles
3	8 miles	10 miles	8 miles	10 miles
4 a.m.	6 miles	4 x 1.5 miles x 100%	6 miles	5 x 1.5 miles x 100%
p.m.	10 x 800m x 100%	6 miles	10 x 800m x 100%	6 miles
5	8 miles	6 miles	8 miles	6 miles
6	6 miles	4 miles	6 miles	4 miles
7	TIME TRIAL*	RACE	TIME TRIAL**	RACE

Total Weekly Mileage

	55-60 miles	55-60 miles	55-60 miles	55-60 miles

All distance running during the competitive phase of training should be performed at 70-80% VO$_2$ max. Rest intervals between the intermittent work bouts should be 1.5 to 2.0 times the duration of the exercise time.

* Time Trial should be 75% of the competitive distance.
** Denotes that time trial should be 1.0-1.25 times the competitive distance.

A Scientific Approach to Distance Running

NUTRITIONAL PREPARATION: EVENTS TAKING ONE HOUR OR MORE

As we pointed out earlier, one of the causes for exhaustion in events like the marathon is the depletion of glycogen from the working muscles. Studies in the early 1960's demonstrated that it was possible to improve endurance performance by increasing the muscle's storage of carbohydrate (glycogen). Several dietary regimens have been recommended to elevate the muscle glycogen stores above the "normal" level of 80 to 100m moles/kg of muscle. I am often asked, "Is the combination of heavy exercise and a high fat/protein diet essential to carbohydrate loading?" My answer is "no."

The keys to success in maximal glycogen loading are (1) to reduce the intensity and duration of your training runs to minimize the daily burn-off of both muscle and liver glycogen stores, and (2) to increase the percentage of carbohydrates in your diet. It may be true that training hard and abstaining from carbohydrates for several days before you start the carbohydrate loading procedure may stimulate a somewhat higher glycogen storage, but I have my doubts. First, the psychological trauma associated with carbohydrate starvation and hard training can unbalance the psychological state of even the most dedicated runners. More important, you should realize that eating a high carbohydrate diet and light training for two or three days is sufficient to elevate your muscle glycogen levels well above normal. In general, most rested distance runners and cyclists have muscle glycogen values of 150 to 250m moles/kg of muscle, roughly 2 to 3 times the level found in untrained muscle and equal to the values normally reported for "carbohydrate loaded" muscle.

Well, then, what diet-rest regime should you use in preparing for long endurance performances? Like all other aspects of the running game, what works for everyone else probably will not work for you. On the average, little running and a high carbohydrate diet for 2 or 3 days should be adequate to maximize your glycogen stores. In my own case, however, I know from repeated muscle biopsies that it takes me 5 to 7 days to fully benefit from the taper.

*Portions of this section have been published in the July 1978 issue of *Runners World.*

How can you judge that your muscles are loaded with glycogen? Since roughly 3 grams of water are stored with each gram of glycogen, carbohydrate loading causes a sudden rise in your body weight. By recording your body weight each morning after you get up and urinate, you will have a good indication of any abrupt changes in body water. If after a couple of days rest, your weight does not rise, then it may suggest that your muscle and liver have not taken on a full load of glycogen. When glycogen loaded your weight should be 1.0 to 3 pounds above your usual training weight.

What form of carbohydrate is best suited for carbohydrate loading? Using radioisotopes to mark different types of sugar molecules, we have found that nearly all the simple (glucose and fructose) and complex sugars (sucrose) begin to appear in the blood as glucose about 5 to 7 minutes after ingestion. Although much has been written concerning the benefits and disadvantages of different types of sugar molecules, to the best of our knowledge they are all delivered to the muscles as glucose. So, it makes little difference what type of sugar you eat; they all produce similar insulin and blood glucose responses. Starches, on the other hand, are absorbed from the gut more slowly and elevate the blood glucose levels for a longer period of time. I am not sure what this means in terms of muscle glycogen storage, but I personally find greater success in carbohydrate loading with pasta feedings than after eating equal amounts of sugary foods (e.g., candy, soft drinks, etc.). Hopefully, our current research projects will tell us more about the types of carbohydrates that are best for carbohydrate loading.

Once you have successfully loaded the muscle and liver with glycogen, we can move on to the problem of what to eat in the hours leading up to the race. Actually it is not a matter of what to eat, but when to eat it. The pre-race meal should be taken no less than three hours before the start. Its contents can include almost anything that will empty rapidly from your stomach. That will, of course, exclude slowly digestible proteins (principally meat) and fatty foods. The idea is to have as little in the stomach as possible when the race starts. In 3 to 4 hours, a stack of pancakes will generally be emptied into the intestine, but meat can be found in the stomach 10 to 12 hours after a meal. Thus, eat cereal, juice, or whatever, but make it a light feeding.

The next critical time zone to consider in the nutritional

preparation for the race is from 15 to 60 minutes before the start. In the past two and one half years we have found some *definite* do's and don'ts that can enhance or impair your performance in long events. First, let's consider the "do's."

As I mentioned earlier, the depletion of muscle glycogen is a primary cause for exhaustion and may, in part, be responsible for the "wall" experienced by many runners at 20 miles. It then follows that performance might be improved if we could find an alternate source of fuel for the muscles to burn instead of glycogen. Such an alternative is fat. Although the runner's highly trained muscles are capable of using fat to produce energy, not enough fat is available to the muscle in its usable form of free fatty acid until relatively late in the run when glycogen stores have already been substantially reduced. We have demonstrated that when exercising muscles are presented with elevated levels of free fatty acids at the beginning of a run, they will burn principally fat and spare muscle glycogen (1).

The obvious question then is, "How can we cause the fat cells to release more free fatty acids?" One simple way is to stimulate the sympathetic nervous system by ingesting caffeine 60 minutes before exercise. As a result of drinking coffee containing 4-5 milligrams of caffeine per kilogram of body weight (roughly two cups of coffee), we have observed 19% increase in exercise time to exhaustion (2). In a more recent study we found that taking a similar caffeine drink before a two hour exercise bout produced a 7% increase in the amount of work that could be performed. Although the subjects had no idea what they were drinking, in every case they found the exercise markedly easier after the caffeine feeding.

What can all this mean to the distance runner? It suggests that a 2:30 marathoner could improve his/her performance by 10 minutes. If you're like me, a 3:30 marathon could turn into a 3:15 fun run. That's not to say a 2:10 marathoner is going to run 2:01 after drinking coffee. To run that fast I am sure such a runner must already have the ability to release large amounts of free fatty acids from his fat cells, and thus might not respond as dramatically to caffeine. We will have to wait in judgment on that theory until more evidence is in. If you want to give the caffeine a try, take a *strong* (about double strength) cup of caffeinated coffee 60 minutes before a 10 mile training run and see how you feel. After you have tried four or five of these runs with and without the coffee, you should be able to decide whether it works for you or not.

It should be noted that caffeine may have some adverse side effects. In hot weather, when dehydration may be a problem, excessive coffee drinking can stimulate the production of urine and subsequent loss of body water. This should not be a problem if you only take coffee once, 60 minutes before the run. The second problem is that there are wide variations in the individual sensitivities to caffeine. Some small individuals are easily overdosed with caffeine and will perform no better than without it. This usually occurs when the dose is greater than 5 mg of caffeine per kilogram of body weight. We have only seen this happen twice, but in both cases the subjects were small females weighing about 50 kilograms.

Now let's consider a nutritional "no, no." In the final hour before the race, don't eat or drink anything that has much sugar in it. This would include such things as candy, pasteries, ice cream, dried fruits, honey, soft drinks, and even athletic drinks. The reason for this is not that sugar is poison or "unnatural," but that when sugars are ingested and absorbed into the blood stream, they quite normally stimulate the release of insulin from the pancreas and reduce the amount of glucose that is normally released from the liver. Insulin does this by accelerating the removal of glucose from the blood by transporting it into the cells of the body. Coincidentally, exercise does the same thing, even in the absence of insulin.

So, what happens when a runner has elevated his blood insulin by eating sugars and then begins to exercise hard? The combination of high insulin and muscular activity causes glucose to be removed from the blood at a rate faster than either the intestine or liver can provide it. As a result, blood glucose may fall from a normal value of 90-100 mg/100 ml to 35-40 mg/100 ml in the first 5 to 10 minutes of exercise. The consequence of this response is that the exercising muscles are suddenly deprived of an important source of fuel, blood sugar, and must now rely more heavily on the next most available source of energy, muscle glycogen. Very simply, eating sugars in the hour preceding exercise will lead to hypoglycemia (low blood sugar) and a greater burning of muscle glycogen. The practical consequence of this is that performance in endurance events may be significantly impaired (3). Our test subjects consistently fatigued earlier and found the running more difficult when they took a sugar drink 30-45 minutes before exercise.

Once the exercise has been initiated, however, the

pancreatic release of insulin is suppressed and will not be affected by sugar feedings. Thus, taking sugar drinks during the exercise will not produce the effects described above, and may even assist the working muscles by providing some of the glucose that normally would only have been available from the liver.

In the preceding discussion I have tried to bring you up to date on a few of the newer findings relative to the nutritional preparation for endurance exercise. Although much nutritional advice may appear theoretically sound, there is little experimentally documented evidence to help you judge what and when to eat. Nevertheless, an understanding of how the body selects and uses fuels, and one's own knowledge of how one feels and performs, will provide the final judgment on the diet best suited for one's competitive preparation.

PREPARATION FOR PERFORMANCE

The simple role of training is to prepare the runner for competition. With that in mind it is important that care be taken to ensure that the runner derive the full benefit of his/her training efforts. Too often the runner's competitive performances fail to exhibit the quality of running exhibited during training. The following discussion, therefore, is aimed at preparing the runner for optimal performance.

Since "peak" performances require a sharpening of both physical and psychological tolerance to the stress of running, the runner should be permitted some relief from the chronic stress of training. In the competitive phase of training, therefore, several days of light training should precede each race. As shown in Table 4-2, the three days before competition are limited to easy endurance running at 60-70% VO_2 max. Such light training minimizes the use of muscle and liver glycogen and ensures the availability of energy during the race. It is during this three-day period that the runner must increase his/her dietary intake of carbohydrates to permit maximal glycogen storage. These efforts to stockpile glycogen should be used only in preparation for competition, but not before a training time trial.

Some coaches advocate complete rest on the day before a race. This procedure is often to the dissatisfaction of the runner, and is really unnecessary. If the run is performed at a relatively slow pace (less than 65% VO_2 max) and does not exceed 4 to 6 miles, then the quantity of glycogen used will be small, thereby having little effect on energy stores. Since recovery from heavy training and glycogen storage requires at least 24 to 48 hours, it is important to realize that one day of rest or light exercise is inadequate preparation for a race. All aspects of the competitive training phase are important to the runner's preparation for performance. There is no purpose in competing with less than full preparation.

In each series of competitive races, the runner will generally experience a peak performance. Such peaks are assumed to be the simultaneous sharpening of both physiological and psychological capacities. The ability to retain this fine edge of performance requires good judgment on the part of both the runner and coach. With proper rest and moderate training, the runner can repeat the quality of performance several times over a three- to four-week period. If for some reason, however, there is an increase in either physical or psychological stress, the "peak" may be lost. Often when the runner performs below a previous best, there is a tendency to increase the training load. The result is a greater loss in the quality of performance. Relief from stress is essential for optimal performance.

Attempts to achieve a peak performance at a specific time adds another dimension to the art of coaching the distance runner. The principles used to prepare a runner for competition are also applicable to producing the peak performance. Tapering the exercise intensity over a period of two weeks is essential for achieving an optimal performance. During that period the runner should refrain from competition and should perform all intermittent workouts at slightly faster than racing pace, with rest intervals that are roughly twice as long as the exercise bouts. The general concept here is to permit the runner to perform "quality" running without undue stress. In the days preceding the competition the usual methods are again employed to ensure adequate glycogen storage.

It should be noted at this point that this system of tapering for peak performance may only prove useful once in a competitive season. The resulting quality performance can, however, be maintained for several weeks as previously described. Inevitably the peak performance will be lost and can only be revived again after a period of basic (non-competitive) training and relief from the psychological stress of competition.

MANAGING THE RUNNER
DURING COMPETITION

Obviously the tactics of competition are more a matter of artistic strategies than of scientific fact. Nevertheless, there are several points of information that may aid the runner in designing a competitive "battle plan." First, it should be remembered that the primary source of energy during the early stage of a race will be the glycogen stored in the muscles. If the pace is unusually fast in the first few minutes of a race, the quantity of glycogen used will be markedly greater and the muscle stores seriously depleted. At the same time, the by-products of rapid glycogen usage may result in a large production of lactic acid, thereby increasing the acid content of the muscle fibers. For these reasons it is wise to run a bit slower than the desired racing pace during the minutes immediately following the start, and to gradually accelerate to racing pace (between the third and fifth minutes of running). Although this plan may be impractical in short races like the 10,000 meters, it can afford a sizeable glycogen sparing effect in races of 10 miles or more. This tactic can minimize the threat of glycogen depletion and lessen the chance for premature exhaustion during the final stage of the race.

The relative rate of energy expenditure (% VO_2 max) during the race is responsible for the runner's sensations of effort and ultimately dictates his/her running pace. Nonetheless, it is important to conserve energy and to run efficiently. Although little attention has been given to the biomechanical aspects of distance running, this topic has been discussed in some detail elsewhere (see: Slocum, D.B. and W. Bowerman. The Biomechanics of Running. *Clin. Orthop.* 23:39-45, 1962). There is evidence to support the tactic of running in the aerodynamic shadow of one's competitor, since the energy needed to overcome the resistance of air increases with the cube of the running velocity or headwind resistance. To gain full advantage of this technique, it is best to permit two or three runners to "break" the wind and to stay within a meter of this leading group.

During races lasting 60 minutes or more it is wise to consider the value of fluid replacement. As discussed earlier (Chapter 2) water intake can significantly reduce the hazards of overheating provided drinks are consumed at frequent intervals. During competition in warm weather, the runner should drink 400-500 milliliters of water thirty minutes before the start of the race. Frequent fluid feeding of 100-200 ml every 15 minutes will minimize dehydration and the risk of overheating.

One final tactical point is the fact that during the latter stage of the race, care should be taken to reserve one's finishing sprint until the final 150-200m. Although it may seem tactically wise to increase the pace to break free of a competitor, the runner should always sense a capacity for additional reserve. Such timing is supported by our knowledge of the muscles' stored ATP-CP. It is these high energy phosphate bonds that permit the explosive energy needed for an all-out sprint. During the final dash, CP decreases rapidly, followed by a fall in muscle ATP. The trick is to begin the final sprint as early as possible without running out of energy short of the finish. If the runner's pace has permitted him/her to achieve a relatively steady state, then the muscle ATP-CP stores are generally sufficient to sustain a sprint lasting roughly 20-30 seconds.

SUMMARY

The preceding discussion provides a number of general and specific principles that are applicable to the training programs of runners having varied abilities and running experience. Certainly our limited knowledge of individual variations in response to training preclude any thought of outlining a single training regimen that will satisfy the needs of all runners. The points most heavily stressed here have been the importance of (1) a long-term progression of training, (2) a balance between work and rest, (3) a balance between speed and endurance running, and (4) proper preparation for peak performance.

Finally, our knowledge of cellular adaptation to endurance training offers us an opportunity to speculate on the training requirements of future champions. It seems that those who are able to train frequently at speeds and distances which approximate the physical demands of competition will acquire the specific adaptations necessary for the ultimate of human endurance. The severity of these training requirements will, of course, be limited by inherent physical qualities, the risk of fatigue-type injuries, the need for rest, and the absence of a center for pain in the central nervous system.

REFERENCES

1. Costill, D.L., E. Coyle, G. Dalsky, W. Evans, W. Fink, and D. Hoopes. Effects of elevated plasma FFA and insulin on muscle glycogen usage during exercise. *J. Appl. Physiol.* 43:695-699, 1977.
2. Costill, D.L., G.P. Dalsky, and W.J. Fink. Effects of caffeine ingestion on metabolism and exercise performance. *Med. Sci. Sports.* (In Press).
3. Foster, C., D.L. Costill and W.J. Fink. Effects of preexercise feedings on endurance performance. *Med. Sci. Sports.* (In Press).

A Scientific Approach to Distance Running